W9-BUI-579

A Testament to the Wilderness

A Testament to the Wilderness

C.A. Meier

Mokusen Miyuki
Joseph L. Henderson
Laurens van der Post
Ian Player
M. Vera Bührmann
Rix Weaver
Jane Hollister Wheelwright
Sam Francis
Robert Hinshaw

Daimon Verlag   The Lapis Press   1985
Zürich   Santa Monica

About this book:

A Testament to the Wilderness was conceived in honor of Prof. C.A. Meier's 80th birthday, April 1985, without his knowledge by a planning committee consisting of Joan Meier, Lela Fischli, Sam Francis and Robert Hinshaw. The book is a cooperative effort of the Daimon Verlag in Zurich and The Lapis Press in Santa Monica, and it appears in two forms: as a limited hardbound deluxe edition and as a paperback, the content of both of which is identical. Copyrights to the essays are retained by the authors.

Typography by Jack W. Stauffacher, The Greenwood Press.

Printed by Christopher Stinehour and Lester R. Ferriss.

Jacket printed by Graham Mackintosh.

ISBN: (hardbound) 0-932499-12-0
       (softbound) 0-932499-13-9

Table of Contents

Robert Hinshaw

Foreword

From the very beginning, it was clear that this volume
in honor of C.A.Meier's 80th birthday was not to be a
testimonial to the past, but rather a living work in itself;
certainly with a special significance for those familiar
with Meier's life and work, but potentially meaningful
for others as well.

Unbeknownst to him, the book grew to its present
form from a seed planted by C.A.Meier himself: one of
his most recent and widely relevant works–his essay
entitled "The Wilderness and the Search for the Soul
of Modern Man," which had been presented at the Third
World Wilderness Congress in Inverness, Scotland, in
October of 1983–was taken as a starting point and sent
to selected colleagues and acquaintances throughout the
world. These friends, all of whom are authorities in their
respective fields, and all of whom have unique relationships with nature and wilderness, were asked to read the
essay and then to respond with original essays addressing
this same topic of the wilderness.The potential contributors were well-acquainted with C.A.Meier's previous
work and he with theirs.

That such a group of outstanding persons from throughout the world—Australia, Japan, Africa, North America, Europe—all gave their best efforts to write original contributions is not only a unique testament to the importance and universality of the theme of wilderness, but also an impressive sign of gratitude and affection for the man to whom this volume is dedicated. All of the contributors, whose "gifts" without exception are reflective of the depths of their long years of life experience, are warmly thanked for their participation.

C.A. Meier has always been an active outdoorsman in his private life, for example, as an avid swimmer, rower and mountain climber. In his professional work, he has not been as directly involved with outer nature as certain of the other participants in this book, though he was passionately interested in the natural sciences as a young boy and later wanted to study marine biology. Depth psychology and marine biology have more in common than might at first meet the eye and, as his "wilderness" article illustrates, C.A. Meier's path through medicine and psychiatry has never really been far from those early interests. Only the means of applying his knowledge and energies has varied, just as the different contributors to this volume reveal individual variations in their approaches to a common topic. *A Testament to the Wilderness* thus both honors and exemplifies the many complementary viewpoints and approaches to the psyche and to nature: in particular, to the wilderness, within and without.

The essays vary greatly in their origins, in emphasis and style, yet they share a reverence for something they all know as "wilderness." Interestingly and, I think,

appropriately, no one pretends to offer an exclusive definition of exactly what wilderness is. Though the central
theme of this book, it still retains its natural mysterious-
ness and each of us is left with our own sense of the con-
tradictions and secrets of nature's unique "order."

I was visiting at a small farm in the south of France in
the early days of 1985 when many of the essays in this
collection were submitted by their authors and I was
reading them for the first time. And during that period
I had an experience which helped to remind me of how
the wilderness is all around us, even in our daily lives.

The Dordogne is an area of very mild climate–usually!
But this January it became unseasonably cold and, what's
more, it *snowed*, a rare event. And then it snowed some
more, and still more, and became *very* cold. The land was
paralyzed: newscasters referred to it as a *"catastrophe
nationale."*

Although the actual quantity of snow wasn't great at
all by central European standards, the *unaccustomedness*
to its being there–and of course to the accompanying
cold–lent it an extraordinary importance. In most cases,
it proved to be a hardship: schools were closed because
the buses were unable to move on the roads (road-clearing
devices were non-existent in this part of the country),
there was no mail delivery, the water mains froze and
burst, the electricity failed repeatedly, and so on.

Nature had the upper hand for several days and we
were thrown back to the tried-and-true methods not only
of heating by direct fire, but also traveling on foot,
melting snow for water and, in general, living almost
exclusively within the microcosm of the immediate neigh-
borhood. The macrocosm, as brought to us in large part

by electronic communication devices, seemed to become abstract, unreal.

It was interesting for me—a visitor, and a northerner more accustomed to yearly rounds of such weather conditions—to observe the reactions and the attitudes taken by the people faced with this out-of-the-ordinary situation: they ranged from bitter feelings of disbelief, victimization, fear and helplessness, to wonder and excitement. This appeared to me to be consistent with the universal human reactions toward wilderness, not only in terms of nature and anomalies of the weather, but also in a broader sense as experienced, for example, in the unexpected, unfamiliar, uncontrollable or unknown, in any form. Whether such a situation is felt as a victimization or a blessing can often be a matter of choice; but which attitude is taken, and why? It seems to me that it has a lot to do with whether one is trying to *master* wilderness, in whatever mode, or is accepting living "within" it; i.e., accepting that human control is perhaps not all that it would like to be, and that we are but a small part of something far greater.

Those who take to camping, hiking, mountain climbing or certain other outdoor activities are usually seeking encounters of one sort or another with "the great outdoors," and this of course involves their inner natures as well. But when such confrontations are forced upon us—whether inwardly, through psychological "crises," outwardly, as in the example mentioned, or by combinations thereof— there is no longer a choice, except with regard to our way of reacting; in any case, we are forced to make adaptations.

On the fourth morning after the snows had begun, the weather cleared and I ventured forth for a walk across field and forest in the strangely white countryside. A whole new world had become visible: the tracks of the unseen creatures of the surroundings were now imprinted everywhere. I followed the meandering trail of a small rabbit until it led to a patch of briar; the sweeping tail of the local fox, well-known for his expertise in raiding the neighboring chicken roost, left behind evidence that he, too, was aware of the rabbit's habitat. At one point, the only sound to be heard was the sonorous tapping of a woodpecker, hard at work, carpenterlike, on the rotten hulk of an ancient, still-erect cypress tree.

I was aware of how that white blanket of snow had covered all signs on the earth below and left a sparkling white screen, a *tabula rasa* onto which the creatures of the land were scratching their life signs, etching out dramas on their stage in the form of tiny trails; the paths of the showplace of their daily lives had been rendered visible by this unaccustomed white "stuff."

A trail of plucked feathers along one stretch of ground attested to a brutal side of this local wilderness world. Meanwhile, the weather itself had wreaked a kind of "purge" throughout the land: back at the house, for example, we noticed that ever fewer birds were to be seen at the little seed-feeding station of my host, which seemed to indicate that the cold had been too much for many of them. Later, news reports confirmed that similar tragedies had occurred in the human realm: particularly the itinerant and the poor had been vulnerable to the extreme conditions.

Our vulnerability to inner wilderness in its various forms can also bring "deaths" of one kind or another; just as there is sorrow and a reluctance to accept the purges of nature in the wilderness of our outside surroundings, so too are we often reluctant to part with familiar, long-held attitudes and assumptions when confronted, violently or not, with their inappropriateness.

I was reminded of the necessity – and the potential meaning – of *crisis*, both within and without: it can be tragic; and at the same time, it provides us with the possibility of renewal. With the purging of the old, in whatever fashion, place is made for something else. This is a phenomenon which can be observed at all levels of life. One example described in the present volume is the African Xhosa rites, in which any potential healing must be preceded by a purging and the acceptance of a non-ego state.

The familiar-unfamiliar sun was a powerful force when it finally reappeared: it brought warmth and light in a newly-appreciated way, thawing the rigid and easing things back into motion. What a wonderful sense of rejuvenation, freshness and life! It seemed to transform our "crisis" into a celebration of the seasons in mini.

I became aware of the relativity of each of these sets of tracks to an individual experience of a particular surrounding; to a wilderness, if you will, and of this local setting to the millenia of other such worlds throughout the universe.

If we are willing and able to be open to it, then it is often just the un-known, the un-planned, the un-expected, the un-familiar which can best teach us. In the tiny prefix "un-," which so often spells trouble, lies the potential for change, for the new, for the hitherto un-considered, un-imagined, un-realized. Our relationships, ideas, attitudes – everything in our little world moves into a new, an "*un-*" perspective: the old is turned on its head.

Very few of us will ever be able to trek the jungles

with Ian Player or perhaps even visit any of the other surviving outer wildernesses of this earth. But we can discover and develop relationships with the wildernesses immediately around us and inside of ourselves by maintaining a genuine respect for the "other," however threatening it may seem to be.

As C. A. Meier pointed out in his first book some thirty-six years ago, it was the *dignity* accorded by the Greeks to the dream which enabled the door to be opened to the healing wonders in the ancient temples of incubation. But the dream, as one manifestation of inner wilderness, has lost in value in subsequent times and today wilderness–both within and without–is generally not bestowed with much dignity of any kind. It is frequently seen as something to be controlled–"tamed"–disrespected and exploited; and then upon occasion, totally feared.

But where is the sense of dignity and awe that accompanied nature in times past? Those wondrous secrets are still there–but for how much longer? The wilderness falling into disrespect, deteriorating and being destroyed is a reflection of our own fate. May the writings in this volume help us to become more aware of the inner and outer essence of nature–and of ourselves.

C.A.Meier

I   *Wilderness and the Search for the Soul of Modern Man*

First of all I should like to give a definition of "wilderness." Wilderness is nature in her original condition undisturbed, unadulterated by man. Does that mean Paradise? As we know, Paradise has been forbidden to us ever since the original sin, but there is a Jewish legend that says that it had been removed by God and relocated at the end of time. Then it becomes eschatological, Utopia, a goal, or *apokatastasis ton panton* [reestablishment of everything]; indicating that it was originally in order, which brings us to the question of how human interference created disorder. Here we are confronted with the age-old problem of opposites:

> nature vs. culture
> matter vs. spirit
> evil vs. good

with mankind in the middle and having to cope with the tension between them.

In *Genesis*, we are encouraged (or ordered) to make use of everything present and to multiply. We certainly did so, right down to the atom bomb and the population explosion. We have abominably exaggerated this liberty to a point where we are about to extinguish ourselves by behaving as if we ourselves were the *creators*. In other words, we are suffering hubris to an extent that cannot go unpunished. We have made use of the laws of nature in humble obedience to the original commandment: e.g., inventing physics, chemistry and biology as best we could and only up to our own limitations. Where, then, is the mistake or the sin? My humble answer, coming from some fifty years of experience with disordered human beings is, that with all this frantic "progress" in the outer world, and all this terribly lopsided extraversion, we became intoxicated and forgot about our soul.

Then we paid for it: neurosis became the plague of our days, the penalty of modern man for his hubris (and here I am more in my own professional field). Man is estranged from his soul, therefore from his own inner nature, by being lost in the outer world. Excessive inter-ference with *outer* nature creates of necessity disorder of the *inner* nature, for the two are intimately connected.

Here I must request your patience for a somewhat lengthy detour into history. Since we cannot understand ourselves and our motivation without knowing something about our spiritual ancestors, I would like to give you some fragmentary information concerning the spiritual history of these predecessary ideas about wilderness conservation.

According to the pre-Socratics, the universe, man included, was one big organism with many organs, of which mankind was only one. The organs functioned in perfect harmony. This was the belief of Heraclitus and also of Parmenides. For the latter, it had consisted of two components, *neikos* and *philotes*, hatred and love, attraction and repulsion. The result was a cyclic change from one to the other in time, in due course. We were, of course, included in this process (and, aren't we now?) This view already tacitly presupposed the existence of what was later called *sympatheia ton holon* [sympathy of all things], an interrelatedness of all things in the cosmos, an idea which found its fundamental place in the philosophy of Poseidonius (135-50 B.C.).[1] We must admit that as long as this idea prevails, we are peacefully contained in something ever so much bigger than ourselves.

In order to better understand the deeper meaning of sympathy with all things in macrocosm and microcosm, we would have to go into alchemy, Jung's idea of synchronicity, and his speculations on *unus mundus* (Dorneus), as well as the "psychoid" factor of matter, which our space here does not permit. Something of the alchemistic idea of *unus mundus* must have been functioning as the unconscious root of Wendell Wilkie's prophetic message, "One World or No World" (*One World*, 1943), however much it was projected on to the macrocosm by him.

Poseidonius' idea did prevail for many centuries, and was widely discussed, mainly in terms of the relationship between macrocosm and microcosm. Man was conceived of as a small cosmos, containing everything in the world, right up to the stars. We could argue that, if this were not so, how could we ever understand anything out there? Epistemologically, for example, in the case of sympathy, Plotinus says that our perception is only possible through sympathy between subject and object. Or, according to Sextus Empiricus: perception, cognition, understanding are only possible by an outpouring of the macrocosm into the microcosm (us). Porphyrius said that the soul, when it encounters the visible, recognizes itself there as it carries everything within itself and the *all of things* is nothing else than the soul.

I could add many more quotations attesting to this conviction, but will now move to a discussion of another, adjoining aspect of the macrocosm-microcosm relation, which will bring us closer to a more current problem in psychology, i.e. the thorny problem of the relation between the psyche and the soma, physis and psyche— body and soul. (Here we border on the problem of psychosomatic medicine, psychophysical dualism or parallelism, etc., of which we still understand next to nothing. I can say with full conviction, and in regard to teachings of philosophers and theologians, that this inevitably culminates in a religious question.)

It must be understood that the concept of macrocosm-microcosm, from the times of Poseidonius, was never conceived as a pair of opposites, but rather as complements which are related by the aforementioned sympathy. Kepler, in his usual prudent way, spoke of a certain proportionality of the two worlds, and with Poseidonius this relationship includes the macrocosm within Man as we know from Cicero (to whom we owe most of what we know of Poseidonius). With Iamblichus it is exactly this relation that, for example, justifies the function of the priest.[2]

You see that hereby he brings down into us, our microcosm, the macrocosmic-divine actions. However, since we are not the mediators between God and ourselves, we have to be careful not to suffer inflation and in order to prevent this dangerous sickness, to maintain our awe and respect of macrocosm, i.e., Nature. The discussion of the macrocosm-microcosm problem went on and became a fundamental notion of Renaissance philosophy. In it, microcosm became the mirror of the macrocosm, to the extent that the perspective was inverted. The world became a *makranthropos* or *megas anthropos* and man was, therefore, a concentration of everything of importance in the cosmos, thereby indeed bordering on inflation, cf. Pico *Heptaplus* 56 q.v.: *Nam si homo est parvus mundus, utique mundus est magnus homo* [For if man is a small world, then the world is a big man]. In our time psychology would step in and warn: "Watch out, lest you become like God!" In John Scotus Eriugena (De divis. nat. IV, 10, ca. 820) something similar is to be found: *Homo veluti omnium conclusio quod omnia in ipso universaliter comprehenduntur* [Man is the inclusion (or end) of all, since everything is enclosed in him]. And our Swiss, Philippus Aureolus Paracelsus: *Omnia una creata sunt, macrocosmos et homo unum sunt* [Everything was created in One, macrocosm and Man are one]. This was his basic conviction and it most probably accounts for his worldwide success as a man of medicine, for he always tried to bring about this macrocosm-microcosm harmony, loss of which, according to him, accounted for his patients' sicknesses.

When we speak of man as microcosm, we cannot, of course, help but think of the "monads" of Leibnitz. He mentions the term by saying *Le microcosme est un monde en raccourci* [The microcosm is a world in miniature], or *un miroir vivant perpetuel de l'univers* [A perpetual living mirror of the universe]. This idea of the mirror brings us back to psychology. Nikolaus Cusanus had already remarked that the *parvus homo* mirror reflects things (including those of the macrocosm). And this, of course, presupposes consciousness (as later with Leibnitz' "monads"). Consciousness means reflection of things perceived, discrimination over against indiscrimination. We try to learn more and more about those objects and begin to analyze and dissect them, thereby eventually killing them, if they are in fact living beings. In other words, as the natural sciences developed, respect for nature as a whole disappeared. We no longer bring sacrifices to her, we think of having dominated her, and to a large extent we *have* dominated her to a point where the original fear of nature has disappeared. What does inner nature (microcosm) say to that loss of fear? At this point, we find that we have lost something equilibrating, equalizing, healthy, sane and of value, a loss for which we have to pay. Thus, anxiety neurosis has become very widespread, and this has its concrete reasons. With our knowledge of the laws of nature, we brought about its domination to the point of constructing A-bombs, and we became destructive to nature in many ways. The dangerous aspects of nature that kept our forebears watchful and humble have now almost disappeared outside; but they have turned inward (wilderness without–wilderness within!) so that the whole of Western society rapidly approaches the physical and mental cracking point from the inner dangers alone. This is no joking matter for should the outer wilderness disappear altogether, it would inevitably resurrect powerfully from within, whereupon it would immediately be projected. Enemies would be created, and its terrifying aspects would take revenge for our neglect, our lack of reverence, our ruthless interference with that beautiful order of things. The wilderness is by no means chaos, it is most admirably ordered, and organized, quietly and beautifully obeying the laws of nature. In modern terminology, this is called cybernetics, meaning self-regulating. But the father of cybernetics, Norbert Wiener, has already written a book entitled *The Human Use of Human Beings*,[3] meaning that, in spite of all the machines, we must behave according to our level–the human level. And what of the self-regulation of nature, when she is no longer left to herself, when she is excessively interfered with, and too badly wounded to be able to recover? The repercussions of this sacrilege in the psyche of the single human being are unpredictable, but one thing is certain: we are in great danger of losing our humanity as a result of this unrelenting process of destruction. If therefore you equally relentlessly make attempts at preserving the wilderness, you are not only doing something idealistic or ideological, but rather something substantial for the health of men globally.

I shall now return to more fundamental considerations concerning your endeavor. It is one of the basic laws of physics that action equals reaction. When you interfere in some way or another with the wilderness, something will inevitably happen to *you* as a reaction, i.e., to the wilderness within, and vice versa. How can we conceive of this? There is a dichotomy in man: on the one hand, we are just a part of nature, but, on the other, we are different, and that different part of our system tries very hard to understand about the One (cf. Plato, Parmenides, *tauton* [identical], and *thateron* [in the other way]). This natural curiosity of the human would be perfectly innocent in itself if it were not insatiable. For centuries, Christianity has emphasized that a mature man should be completely freed of his natural carnal being. But such a man turns sour! We must learn to live with both natures and with their opposites, and we must also learn to cope with the suffering of this tension. Our inner nature does not tolerate too much interference such as repression, askesis, etc. As there is now this correspondence between the two worlds alluded to earlier on, we must respect this subtle balance. The wilderness within would really go "wild" if we should badly damage the outer wilderness. So let us keep the balance as best we can, in order to maintain sanity.

How can this be practiced? As a psychologist, I am not going to give you technical advice, but I shall try to intimate to you how psychology may help. First of all, we must frankly admit that, in spite of our culture, we are still mammals, natural beings. This aspect of our being, last but not least, is forgotten by that selfsame culture; we are, as we say, unconscious of its archeological, prehistoric existence and reality in the unconscious part of our psyche. Now, everything in us of which we are unconscious, is automatically projected. You only have to think of the primitive fear of animals, whether it be spiders, mice, snakes or tigers, almost all of them being perfectly harmless if left unmolested. But those powers in the unconscious are overwhelming, so that we are tempted to project them as far away as possible, onto the stars, for example, more particularly when we have to deal with fate. And this in spite of the fact that in 1798 Schiller let Illo say to Wallenstein's astrologer Seni: "In your bosom are the stars of your fate."⁴ And, I do not have to tell you how, with the increasing insecurity on this planet, people tend more than ever to believe in this projection of secular astrology. Scientifically those allegedly extremely personal effects of specific stars on Tom, Dick or Harry are inconceivable.

How does the case look when this astrological illusion

is analyzed psychologically? First of all, we have populated the starry sky with a vast collection of gods and myths. Planets are named for the gods. Concerning myths you only have to think of Andromeda, Orion, etc. First of all, we created constellations out of purely statistically distributed single stars; and secondly, we endowed them with mythological names such as Andromeda, Orion, etc. It has become a psychological truism that such images have an archetypal origin, which means that they correspond to certain pre-existing images and processes in our collective unconscious, and therefore get projected. But, however unconscious, they are having their effects upon our behavior, and thus constitute our fate. This projection onto the stars is not altogether harmless, since projection is a psychological reality, an *action*, which consequently has its *reaction* upon us. So this is the way in which these benevolent or malevolent stars or constellations in turn have their effects upon us. We need only remain unconscious of them, and the archetypes go to work, and the boomerang of projection hits back.

The reality of psychological factors is a hard fact, and should no longer be denied in the name of exact science. Archetypes are frighteningly contagious as evidenced by the many mass movements in history. The Huns, Vandals, Turks, French and Russian Revolutions, Napoleonism and Hitler are classic examples of the phenomenon of mass projection. *Plus ça change, plus ça reste la même chose*. [The more things change, the more they remain the same]. It is only the names that change. Suffice it to say, no matter how civilized one may be, identification with an archetype can lead to the megalomania of a ruler of the world, something close to God Almighty.

Concerning the efficacy of projections and the relation of macrocosm and microcosm, I will relate a true story, which to my mind illustrates all this most beautifully. It is the story of the Rain Maker of Kiao Chow, which I owe to Richard Wilhelm. He told us this true story, which he witnessed himself, at the Psychological Club in Zürich.

He lived in a district of China that happened to be threatened with famine and a terrific drought. The inhabitants tried to produce rain with the help of their own local rain makers, processions, etc., but to no avail. So they sent for China's most famous rain maker, who lived far away in Kiao Chow. They asked him what they could do to assist him, but he only wanted a secluded place in the wilderness, where he was to be left alone, except for the delivery of his daily meals.

After a couple of days without rain the people became impatient and sent a delegation to ask him why there was no success, but he simply sent them back. On the next day it began to snow (in mid-summer!) and then the snow turned into pouring rain. On his return to the village, they asked why it had taken him so long. He explained: 'When I came to this district, I immediately realized that it was frighteningly out of Tao, whereby being here myself, I naturally was also out of Tao. All I could do therefore, was to retire into the wilderness (nature) and meditate, so as to get myself back into Tao.' [recall here that Jesus also had to retire into the wilderness whenever he was confronted with a problem that needed meditation]. *With that, the Rainmaker returned to Kiao Chow, happy as a lark.*

You may dismiss this whole event as sheer coincidence, as such things may happen in full accord with the laws of nature once in a blue moon. But snow in mid-summer is still less likely. What is its probability from a purely meteorological point of view? Recalling the story, we can say the following: The magician comes to a place which is physically out of order and notices this immediately, thereby falls out of order himself (being contaminated, taking macrocosm into microcosm, introjecting), so that he becomes a part of unbalanced, sick nature. He then attempts to put himself back in Tao again, which is hard work, but he succeeds. With that, Nature herself is healed, and it rains; in other words, the boomerang hit the target.

Here we have not only a beautiful example of the reestablished harmony of macrocosm and microcosm, but also of the way in which we, the microcosm, are capable of contributing to this harmony, i.e., *corriger la fortune* [of directing our destiny]. The archetypes are *in us*, and some of them represent the *chthonic* part of our soul, by which we are linked to Earth and to Nature. That can certainly be linked to the wilderness.

We are fascinated, as well as afraid of these archetypal components of nature, and so we want to know more about them. Historically speaking, this is a very new attitude which only began to dawn with the Renaissance, as when Petrarch climbed Mont Ventou, thereby becoming the father of mountaineering. Mountains are obviously one kind of wilderness, which ask for many human sacrifices every year. There are other dangerous wildernesses that are just as hostile as mountains: the Arctics and Antarctics with their icy coldness and darkness; the desert with its heat and dryness; the impenetrable jungle; the sea with its frightening storms and unfathomable, briny, dark depths. I assure you, they can all be found in our own depths, in our own unconscious.

The tragedy is that with more and more knowledge of this outer wilderness we cannot tranquilize the inner wilderness. Nature cannot be placated by artifacts. She stands in her own right and will never surrender her position. Why is it that we cannot make peace with her? We have explored macrocosm too extensively, ill-advisedly, and with too much success, and thereby lost sight of the microcosm. The more I think of this quandary, the more I begin to understand humankind's endeavor. It is a much healthier attitude to try to preserve the outer wilderness than to negate the inner wilderness and thereby let it go rampant, whereupon it inevitably becomes projected onto your fellow beings, whether friend or foe. In order to keep in harmony with the concept of Wilderness equaling Nature unspoiled, apart from analysis I know of nothing better than to keep the outer Wilderness alive and to not let it be ruined. Thus, you will find Nature an idyllic landscape where the law of the jungle still holds. For, as long as you don't interfere with it too badly, it functions beautifully. I should like to quote here a famous Persian-Egyptian alchemistic authority (thought to have lived in the fourth century B.C.) by the name of Ostanes.

1.) ἡ φύσις τῇ φύσει τέρπεται
2.) ἡ φύσις τὴν φύσιν νικᾷ
3.) ἡ φύσις τὴν φύσιν κρατεῖ

1.) Nature enjoys Nature;
2.) Nature vanquishes Nature;
3.) Nature rules Nature.

These three lines may sound trivial, but at the same time they are very deep.

1.) Let her be as she is, and she will enjoy herself like a virgin;

2.) she will always be victorious, self-regulated;

3.) she will religiously obey her own rules.

Psychology gives us many good reasons for keeping in touch with the "Wilderness equals Nature" concept:

We live on the upper floor (consciousness). It is supported by the lower one (the unconscious), and eventually by its foundation, the cellar (let's not forget that we also keep wine in the cellar which equals spirit). It represents the unconscious, the earth, our mother, "mother nature" and, when in its original condition, the virgin nature, with which we live in a sort of "participation mystique" (Lévy-Bruhl); it is there that the archetypes live. The archetypes correspond to our instincts, which are the *psychological* aspects of the *biological facts*, the patterns of behavior by which we live and are lived. But, inasmuch as we are unconscious of the archetypes, they are projected, i.e., they are experienced as if they were in the macrocosm. Usually they are personified (bush soul, animals, brother animal–Kipling's *Jungle Book*) and this is how we originally become "related" to animals.

This part of our psyche is thus experienced in the form of outside objects, although it belongs strictly to us, the subject, the microcosm. You need only think of phenomena such as *lykanthropy* (werewolves), which is simply an identification with the animal. On this level of semi-consciousness, there can exist uncanny places in which demons dwell, wells populated with nymphs or djinns; in short, the soul is divided up into many partial souls. So the Wilderness is really the original biotope of the Soul.

With the development of consciousness in our Western civilization, these fragments slowly begin to be integrated, but however strongly we believe in "progress" (of consciousness), a total integration remains a hopeless desideratum. The ideal outcome of it was called *individuation* by Jung. But, alas, the unconscious is as inexhaustible as nature, and as deep as "the deep blue sea." This is our inner wilderness.

I will now return to my favorite idea of the correlation of macrocosm-microcosm, which seems to me to justify beautifully the enthusiasm for conservation of wilderness.

One of the protagonists of this whole idea was Robert Fludd, a humanist who wrote in Latin, and therefore called himself Robertus de Fluctibus (1574-1637). A medical man, Fludd was a Rosicrucian, an alchemist, and an admirer of Paracelsus. He is best known for his battle with Kepler whom he accused of not paying enough attention to the "yeast" (*faex*) in matter. He published many beautifully illustrated books, and most of the excellent etchings by Johann Theodor de Bry therein are concerned with the connection of macrocosm and microcosm. His ideas, as we can see now, go back to Poseidonius, who said that man was a microcosm, having his being in common with stones–his life with plants–his perception with animals–and his reason with the angels. From here, Fludd claimed that we get in touch with the Supreme Being by means of the mediation of Nature (woman), who on the one hand sums up minerals, plants, animals (the ape being their summit), and on the other hand, (*via aurea catena Homeri*) is linked to the ineffable God. There could not be a better example of the harmony of macrocosm-microcosm, mediated by nature in her virginal aspect. Fludd had worked it out in endless detail in most of his many books. As for example, his *Clavis philosophiae et alchymiae* (1633), and *Philosophia Moysaica* (1635). He was by no means alone, but found himself in full accordance with such people as Pico della Mirandola, Girolamo Cardano, Tommaso Campanella, Giordano Bruno and most of the other prominent figures of Renaissance philosophy.

These men were influenced by early Platonic ideas such as the "World Soul," the "Soul of the Universe," and the "Anima Mundi" (*Timaeus* 41D). However, it looks as if Fludd's efforts did not have much of an echo in the world, or if so it is hard to find. But Schopenhauer repeatedly refers to this concept, mainly in his magnum opus (*The World as Will and Representation II*, §29), where he wholly agrees with the macrocosm-microcosm idea, without, however, referring to Fludd.

According to Shaftesbury (1671-1713), the goal of man is to achieve harmony. Shaftesbury has a long prehistory, since a great number of the Fathers of the Church have dealt with the problem of macrocosm-microcosm by discussing Plato's *Anima Mundi*, the *pneuma* of the *Stoa* and Plotinus.

I was always shocked by the Jewish way of dealing with evil: (Leviticus 16.2) loading the scapegoat Azazel with the people's sins and then driving him out into the wilderness to the "Lord of the Flyes." I am sure you won't find *him* there, but rather you will find some of the many healing spirits of Nature! In any case, let us not forget the vandalism against Nature, that is presently afoot. And let us also not forget that only recently even purely scientific ethologists came to believe that one can observe altruistic actions with certain higher animals, so that the origins or phylogeny of ethics are to be found already in unspoiled nature.[5]

I should like to remind you of the way in which Voltaire concludes a long philosophical discussion by letting Candide say: *Cela est bien dit, mais il faut cultiver notre jardin.* [All that is well said, but we must cultivate our own garden.] I only hope not to have destroyed your enthusiasm but rather to have helped you to find something of this harmony and beauty during your outings, and to live it, which is the only way of properly relating to it and loving it. As Rudyard Kipling wrote:

"Good hunting to all
That keep the Jungle Law!"

NOTES

1. cf. Karl Reinhardt, *Kosmos und Sympathie.* Munich, 1926.
2. Iamblichus, Sec. IV, Chapter 2, *On the Mysteries of the Egyptians, Chaldeans and Assyrians,* Thomas Taylor, ed. London, 1895, p. 207: "For these things, also, another reason may be assigned, and which is as follows: in all theurgical operations the priest sustains a twofold character; one, indeed, as man, and which preserves the order possessed by our nature in the universe; but the other, which is corroborated by divine signs, and through these is conjoined to more excellent natures (seq. p. 3), and is elevated to their order by an elegant circumduction, this is deservedly capable of being surrounded with the external form of the Gods. Conformably, thereof, to a difference of this kind, the priest very properly invokes, as more excellent natures, the powers derived from the universe, so far as he who invokes is a man; and again, he commands these powers, because through arcane symbols, he, in a certain respect, is invested with the sacred form of the Gods."
3. Norbert Wiener, *The Human Use of Human Beings: Cybernetics and Society.* London, 1950.
4. Frederic Schiller, *The Piccolomini II* 6, 2069. Compare also what,

more than 100 years earlier, Shakespeare said in *Julius Caesar* I,ii, 139-141: "Men at some time are masters of their fates:/The fault, dear Brutus, is not in our stars/But in ourselves, that we are the underlings."

5. *Live Sciences Report* (9th ed.), Gunter Stent, "Morality as a Biological Phenomenon," Dahlem Konferenzen, Abakon Verlagsgesellschaft Berlin, 1978.

Mokusen Miyuki

2　The Arts of Mr. Hun Tun

First of all I should like to express my sincere congratulations to Professor C. A. Meier on his eightieth birthday. He was my analyst while I was studying at the C. G. Jung Institute in Zürich from 1964 to 1968, and since leaving Zürich for Los Angeles in the fall of 1968, I have never lost contact with him. I have felt his presence in my analytical practice as well, and when giving lectures. Therefore I am grateful for this opportunity to write a response to C. A. Meier's article entitled "Wilderness and the Search for the Soul of Modern Man." This response is personal, but I believe it is also "universal" in that it shares the human concerns Professor Meier expresses in his article and amplifies the theme he attempts to clarify.

"The Arts of Mr. Hun Tun," or "The Chaos," is one of the proverbial stories of Chuang Tzu. While I was reading Professor Meier's article, two images persistently came to me as if they had been responding to his theme "Wilderness equals Nature:" one is the image of an old man practicing the arts of Mr. Hun Tun and the other is that of a dog driving in New York City.

The image of a dog driving in New York is from the dream of H.M., the first analysand I had as a diploma candidate in Zürich. H.M. was then a university student, intellectually gifted yet emotionally "disturbed." He proudly considered himself as *freigeistig* [free-spirited], yet he was suffering from boredom, anxiety, depression and a suicidal impulse. His psychic condition can be seen in the following dream which he brought to our seventh session along with his poem entitled "Atomic Bomb."

My dog Bärli (bear) is driving a car in New York City. People think that the dog is intelligent enough to drive. But I know that Bärli is rather stupid. I don't want to tell the truth to the people enjoying the dog driving because I want to be proud of my dog. To be honest, however, it is quite painful not to tell them the truth. In my view, the dog drives very dangerously, although so far he has driven successfully. I am thinking that soon there will be a catastrophe.

The story of the arts of Mr. Hun Tun is told by Chuang Tzu, an ancient Taoist thinker who is believed to have lived during the fourth century B.C. This story is found in the twelfth chapter of the *Chuang Tzu* entitled "Heaven and Earth."[1] The story is translated by Burton Watson as follows:

Tzu-kung traveled south to Ch'u, and on his way back through Chin, as he passed along the south bank of the Han, he saw an old man preparing his fields for planting. He had hollowed out an opening by which he entered the well and from which he emerged, lugging a pitcher, which he carried out to water the fields. Grunting and puffing, he used up a great deal of energy and produced very little result.

'There is a machine for this sort of thing,' said Tzu-kung.

'In one day it can water a hundred fields, demanding very little effort and producing excellent results. Wouldn't you like one?'

The gardener raised his head and looked at Tzu-kung. 'How does it work?'

'It's a contraption made by shaping a piece of wood. The back end is heavy and the front end light and it raises the water as though it were pouring it out, so fast that it seems to boil right over! It's called a well sweep.'

The gardener flushed with anger then said with a laugh, 'I've heard my teacher say, where there are machines, there are bound to be machine worries; where there are machine worries, there are bound to be machine hearts. With a machine heart in your breast, you've spoiled what was pure and simple; and without the pure and simple, the life of the spirit knows no rest. Where the life of the spirit knows no rest, the Way will cease to buoy you up. It's not that I don't know about your machine—I would be ashamed to use it!'

Tzu-kung blushed with chagrin, looked down and made no reply....

When Tzu-kung got back to Lu, he reported the incident to Confucius. Confucius said: 'He is one of those bogus practitioners of the arts of Mr. Chaos. He knows the first thing but doesn't understand the second. He looks after what is on the inside but doesn't look after what is on the outside. A man of true brightness and purity is one who can enter into simplicity, who can return to the primitive through inaction, give body to his inborn nature, and embrace his spirit, and in this way wander through the everyday world—if you had met one like that, you would have had real cause for astonishment. As for the arts of Mr. Chaos, you and I need not bother to find out about them.'

Although the image of a dog driving in New York and that of an old man practicing the arts of Mr. Hun Tun appear to be unrelated, there is, I believe, a link between these two images which, in turn, is amplificatory to C.A. Meier's contention. I recalled that the dream of H.M. came to me when I read the following passage in C.A. Meier's article:

The dangerous aspects of nature that kept our forebears watchful and humble have now almost disappeared outside; but they have turned inward (wilderness without—wilderness within!) so that the whole of Western society rapidly approaches the physical and mental cracking point from the inner dangers alone. This is no joking matter for should the outer wilderness disappear altogether, it would inevitably resurrect powerfully from within, whereupon it would immediately be projected. Enemies would be created, and its terrifying aspects would take revenge for our neglect, our lack of reverence, our ruthless interference with that beautiful order of things.[2]

The key concept in this quotation is that of projection. According to C.G. Jung, projection is "the expulsion of a subjective content into an object."[3] However, being an unconscious process, the subjective content projected into an object remains unconscious. This means that projection cannot be caused at will; it *happens*, instead, to an individual or group. C.A. Meier has pointed out: "...should the outer wilderness disappear altogether, it would inevitably resurrect powerfully from within, whereupon it would immediately be projected." The reckless dog driving in New York, therefore, can be taken as projection of the psychic wilderness of H.M., whose superb intellect had caused a dangerous psychic imbalance.

In analysis, important dream images, such as that of the "wild" dog of H.M., can be taken on the level of understanding called *subjective*, so that the dreamer is invited to make efforts to amplify the image in question by means of other images, ideas, or feelings associated with similar experiences in his life context. As a matter of fact, the analysis with H.M. took this direction. Thus, he had to reexamine his way of life, which he had proudly characterized as *freigeistig*, or being free from any established values, be they philosophical or religious. Needless to say, his intellect was easily able to justify this characterization. It was rather clear that, for him, to be *freigeistig* was nothing but an act of the ego unduly appropriating his life, both conscious and unconscious. His hubris—that is, the arrogance and narrowness of ego consciousness judging everything by its "pet" standard—resulted in severe interference in his own nature to the extent that he was suffering from the banality of life and a suicidal impulse. H.M. can be regarded as an exemplary modern man described by C.A. Meier as follows:

... *neurosis became the plague of our days, the penalty of modern man for his hubris... Man is estranged from his soul, therefore from his own inner nature, by being lost in the outer world.*[4]

This observation of Professor Meier's invites us to ask an important question: Doesn't the dream of H.M. speak also for the collective neurosis of today? Cannot the hubris and the neurosis of H.M. be regarded as the general condition of the so-called technocratic society? In other words, if the dream of H.M., who is highly intellectual, is understood on the subjective level as speaking for his personal neurosis, due to the overdeveloped "head" at the cost of the "heart," might it not also be understood on the objective level in the wider context of the ills of today?

Interestingly enough, having told me the dream, H.M. picked up his poem entitled "Atomic Bomb" for discussion. I did not expect this and felt strange. The poem is of considerable length, so that we were able to finish only the first third of it. Its major theme was the unbearable banality of life which could be "cured" only by the catastrophe of an atomic explosion. This image might sound destructive as well as pessimistic, yet what H.M. really wanted to communicate was the birth of new life and values after the complete annihilation of the old ones. The decisive reason why the destructive "bombing" is positive for H.M. was that the accidental bombing by the U. S. Air Force of the factories in Zürich during the Second World War had given his mother such a "catastrophic" shock that she delivered him two months earlier than expected. Because his life began two months earlier as a result of the bombing and his mother's fear of catastrophe, H.M. felt somewhat positive about it. However, today, in the age of highly advanced technology, we must ask seriously what kind of hope will be left when nuclear war takes place. In the event of complete destruction as the result of a nuclear exchange, what kind of life will be found?

The issue of the nuclear threat, it seems, is well addressed by the image of the dog recklessly driving in New York, a city representing the capital of technocracy. The hubris of technological man can be symbolized by the "wild" dog as well as by the people who enjoyed the phenomenon of the driving. Unlike the other people in the dream, H.M. feared a catastrophe. On the subjective level, this can be understood as indicating an enrichment and enlargement of the conscious contents through the ego's efforts to get in touch with the unconscious. In other words, the ego became aware of the issue of the over-developed "head" at the cost of the "heart," thus it was separated from the majority.

The image of the dog driving in New York and that of the people who were entertained by the driving dog also helps us raise another serious question on the objective level with regard to the nature of the consciousness of technocratic man: Is not the consciousness of the technocratic man aptly symbolized by the "wild" dog in the sense of being blindly motivated by territorial instinct and conditioned by hunger for survival and power? It seems undeniable that the hubris of modern man, of which Professor Meier speaks, coincides with the dangerous driving of the dog with his inflated "head" who thought he could manage the situation, not realizing the approaching catastrophe. As Professor Meier points out, the wilderness which disappeared into the unconscious has created the threatening situation. Many individuals have been feeling, with Robert Lifton, that after Auschwitz and Hiroshima/Nagasaki, "the potential for victimization and for genocide is not only broadly human, but specifically human."[5]

To make matters worse, there is a prevailing sense of the "unreality" of the vast, complex, artificial structure of technocracy. For many individuals, it is so meaningless to confront and to live in such an "unreal" and opaque world of technical civilization that they feel alienated, fragmented, and not at all integrated. Sam Keen, an American thinker who expresses concern for society's ills, maintains that modern *homo faber* suffers from the "spiritual schizophrenia" oscillating "between

omnipotent and impotent feelings and expectations."[6]
The dream of H.M. also shows this suffering of *homo faber* as it constitutes two poles, the people having confidence in the dog's intelligence and H.M., who is fearful of a catastrophe.

It goes without saying that the ills of today, whether they be a nuclear threat or that of fragmented, meaningless life, are man-made, man being *homo faber*. As C.A. Meier maintains, the image of man as *homo faber*, planning, controlling and manipulating, can be traced back to the Biblical image of man in Genesis. Being created in God's image, *homo faber* has insisted that it is God's will to plan, control, and manipulate nature for his proper ends. The "divine" mission thus carried out by *homo faber* has brought about materialistic prosperity on the one hand, yet on the other it has resulted in the exploitation and destruction of nature both within and without. Thus, *homo faber* has been facing the danger of spiritual fragmentation within, as well as ecological crisis and nuclear extinction without. As Professor Meier enjoins us, it is time for *homo faber* to turn his eyes to the inner reality of the psyche and to look for a new myth which may help him bring about a new orientation in life. It is this issue, I believe, that the Taoist myth of the arts of Mr. Hun Tun addresses.

The old man preparing his field for planting does appear as silly as the dog driving in New York. According to Confucius, the old man is "one of those bogus practitioners of the arts of Hun Tun." Nevertheless, what the old man said made a great impact on Tzu-kung and unexpectedly caused him to reflect on the way he was living. It is known that Confucius also taught Tao in terms of *jen*, or human-heartedness, emphasizing the cultivation of purity of heart and simplicity of life. I believe this is the reason that Chuang Tzu has Confucius explain the arts of Mr. Hun Tun to Tzu-kung. With the inclusion of this Taoistic element, the story clarifies the issue of the common ground shared by Confucianism and Taoism.

At this point, I would like to explore the implications of the old man's reasoning. The idea that he would consciously choose the most painstaking method to prepare his field for planting speaks to the same emphatic conclusion regarding the detrimental effects that the mechanized, technological world has upon the psyche that C. A. Meier presents in "Wilderness and the Search for the Soul of Modern Man."

In my understanding, the words of the old farmer are based on Professor Meier's "favorite idea of the correlation of macrocosm-microcosm;" hence, it could be taken as amplificatory to "The Story of the Rain Maker of Kiao Chow" which he utilizes to discuss "the efficacy of projection and the relation of macrocosm and microcosm."

Furthermore, this exploration attempts to articulate what can be called the "feminine functioning of the ego," in contrast to the ego's masculine functioning as seen in the case of the *homo faber*, a planner, controller, or manipulator. The ego's feminine functioning, as Confucius appropriately terms it, is an art, as in the case of the arts of Mr. Hun Tun, and is well related to the healing process of nature within and without, which the story of the Rain Maker conveys.

The old gardener's words call to mind an expression of Professor Meier's, the danger of "the human interference." It is common knowledge that Taoists, such as Lao Tzu or Chuang Tzu, have been critical of the dangerous aspect of human contrivance. In his *Commentary on the Secret of the Golden Flower*, Jung perceptively comments on the basic Taoist principle *wu wei:*

Now and then it happened in my practice that a patient grew beyond himself because of unknown potentialities, and this became an experience of prime importance to me. In the meantime, I had learned, that the greatest and most important problems of life are all fundamentally insoluble. They must be so for they express the necessary polarity inherent in every self-regulating system. They can never be solved, but only outgrown....The new thing came to them from obscure possibilities either outside or inside themselves; they accepted it and grew with its help.... *But the new thing never came exclusively either from within or from without....*

What did these people do to bring about the development that set them free? As far as I could see they did nothing (wu wei) *but let things happen. As Master Lü-tsu teaches in our text, the light rotates according to its own law, if one does not give up one's ordinary occupation.* The art of letting things happen, *action through non-action, letting go of oneself as taught by Meister Eckhart, became for me the key that opens the door to the way. We must be able to* let things happen in the psyche. *For us, this is an art of which most people know nothing. Consciousness is forever interfering, helping, correcting, and negating, never leaving the psychic processes to grow in peace....*(The emphasis is mine.) 7

In his commentary, Jung clearly emphasizes the importance of the attitude of acceptance for letting things happen and allowing them to take their own course, both within and without the psyche. It also should be noted that Jung contrasts this attitude of wu wei to that of interfering consciousness. These two attitudes, receptive and interfering, can be understood in conjunction with Jung's concepts of *introvert* and *extrovert*, respectively. The psychic energy flows toward the "within" (subject) in the case of acceptance, while it goes toward the "without" (object) in the case of interference. Nevertheless, I would like to designate these two attitudes "feminine" and "masculine" according to the way the ego functions. Both the Rain Maker and the old gardener are aware of what Jung terms *unknown possibility*, so that for each, the ego-consciousness is able to become receptive to it and to function in the "feminine" receptive manner, in contrast to the "masculine" aggressive functioning. In traditional Chinese terminology, the feminine functioning can be termed *yin* and the masculine *yang*–both yin and yang being the manifested function of Tao of *coincidentia oppositorum*.

The function of Tao as *coincidentia oppositorum* is best formulated, in my view, in the "Appended Remarks" of the *I Ching*, in terms of Tao as *i-yin i-yang*, which literally means "one yin (and) one yang." Richard Wilhelm's translation reads: "That which lets now the dark, now the light appear is Tao."[8] The same passage is translated by James Legge as follows: "The successive movement of the inactive and active operations constitutes what is called the course [of things]."[9] As these translations communicate, the function of Tao lies in uniting the opposites by balancing them. Hence, an excessive operation of the yang or masculine ego leads to a state of imbalance and destruction. The old farmer's refusal to employ a machine to prepare his field for planting and his words to Tzu-kung illustrate this fear and his particular emphasis upon the ego's feminine functioning.

Needless to say, a precise translation of one language into another is quite difficult, if not impossible. This is all the more so with any scholar's attempt to translate Chinese into English or other European languages. Therefore, it is necessary here to examine the terms H.A. Giles used in translating what B.Watson translated as "machine," "machine worries," and "machine heart." Giles's translations are "cunning implements," "cunning in their dealings" and "cunning in their hearts"[10] respectively, thus indicating the manipulating act of the ego's masculine functioning. A man's heart or human concern would be lost by using machines or implements for more profitable productivity, which is connected with success, competition, or possession–to which the ego's masculine acts of planning, control and manipulation are directed. In this manner, man would lose human worries or concerns, as well as hearts, and as a result, he would be transformed into a machine with a machine heart, thus losing the purity and simplicity of the heart–which coincides with the function of Tao, of yin-yang.

The loss of the heart's purity and simplicity, therefore, means the loss of connection with Tao's activity. In B.Watson's translation, the old man says:

...with a machine heart in your breast, you've spoiled what was pure and simple; and without the pure and simple, the life of the spirit knows no rest. Where the life of the spirit knows no rest, the Way will cease to buoy you up....

The same passage is translated by H.A.Giles as follows:

...those who have cunning in their hearts cannot be pure and incorrupt, and that those who are not pure and incorrupt are restless in spirit, and those who are restless in spirit are not fit vehicles for Tao.[11]

The Chinese expression for "the life of the spirit knows no rest" in B. Watson's translation and "restless in spirit" for H. A. Giles is *shen sheng pu ting*, which can be translated literally as "the birth/emergence of *shen* becomes unfocused." The key term in this passage is *shen* which is defined in the "Appended Remarks" of the *I Ching* as "that which is unfathomable in the operation of yin and yang." [12] This term *shen* is usually translated as *spirit*, as both B. Watson and H. A. Giles have done, but it clearly refers to the function of Tao in terms of *i-yin i-yang*, which we have discussed above. Speaking of the unfathomableness of Tao's function, Chuang Tzu elsewhere states that "The Way [Tao] gathers in emptiness [*hsü*] alone. Emptiness is the fasting of the mind [*hsin-chi*]." [13] Therefore, the Chinese expression *shen sheng pu ting* means that the function of Tao becomes unfocused when the ego's contrivance takes place and that, accordingly, Tao's emergence does not occur.

In Chuang Tzu's collected works there is a classic story which shows the danger of the human interference, or the excessive functioning of the ego in the masculine manner. Thus we learn of the death of Hun Tun:

The emperor of the South Sea was called Shu [Brief], the emperor of the North Sea was called Hu [Sudden], and the emperor of the central region was called Hun-tun [Chaos]. Shu and Hu from time to time came together for a meeting in the territory of Hun-tun, and Hun-tun treated them very generously. Shu and Hu discussed how they could repay his kindness. 'All men,' they said, 'have seven openings so they can see, hear, eat and breathe. But Hun-tun alone doesn't have any. Let's try boring him some!'

Everyday they bored another hole, and on the seventh day

Hun-tun died.[14]

Marie-Louise von Franz, a noted Jungian analyst, views this story as "exceedingly meaningful" because it "mirrors the questionable aspects of our civilization with its over-evaluation of craft, technology, and consciousness."[15] Note here that the two terms *shu* and *hu* are used interchangeably in the sense of heedless, sudden, hasty, ceaseless, or unexpected, which can duly describe the dangerous manipulating by the *homo faber* of nature, technology, or politics. Hun Tun can be taken as symbolic for the unconscious as the creative matrix of life, which is killed by the act of conscious interference represented by the two emperors, Shu and Hu. This myth of "de-creation" seems to speak well for the fearful situation we face today with the threat of total nuclear destruction and ecological crisis.

Nearly forty years ago, in 1946, C.G. Jung seriously warned us of the nuclear threat:
The conflagration that broke out in Germany was the outcome of psychic conditions that are universal. The real danger signal is not the fiery sign that hung over Germany, but the unleashing of atomic energy, which has given the human race the power to annihilate itself completely. The situation is about the same as if a small boy of six had been given a bag of dynamite for a birthday present.[16]
Jung was afraid of "the outcome of psychic conditions that are universal," which he compared to that of "a small boy of six . . . given a bag of dynamite for a birthday present." This image of the modern *homo faber* coincides with that of the "wild" dog driving proudly in New York as well as that of the two emperors, Shu and Hu, who "happened" to kill Hun-tun, ironically, out of inno-

cent good will and appreciation. Without fail, the old gardener would say that it is the price *homo faber* must pay for his excessive interference with nature, neglecting, as he does, the purity and simplicity of the heart which functions together with Tao. It is, then, of primary importance for *homo faber* to cultivate the feminine way of ego functioning, although it may appear somewhat nonsensical for the masculine ego and will certainly require painstaking work.

In this vein, I am reminded of another story about Jung. Some eight years after he warned us of the nuclear threat, Jung spoke again on the subject at the Zürich Psychological Club. Barbara Hannah, a Jungian analyst and author, recalls the scene:

About 1954 he [Jung] was asked at a discussion in the Zürich Psychological Club, whether he thought there would be an atomic war and if so what would happen. He replied: 'I think it depends on how many people can stand the tension of the opposites in themselves. If enough can do so, I think the situation will just hold, and we shall be able to creep around innumerable threats and thus avoid the worst catastrophe of all: the final clash of opposites in an atomic war. But if there are not enough and such a war should break out, I am afraid it would inevitably mean the end of our civilization as so many civilizations have ended in the past but on a smaller scale.' [17]

The individuals who Jung says "can stand the tension of the opposites in themselves" are those whose egos function in the feminine way, countering the over-developed masculine ego, and allowing the unfathomable operation of the Tao, of yin-yang, to take place. Their egos "let things happen in the psyche," in contrast to the masculine functioning ego which is "forever interfering, helping, correcting, and negating, and never leaving the simple growth of the psychic processes in peace."[18]

"To let things happen," or wu wei in Taoist terminology, does not coincide with masculine ego functioning–planning and interfering. Therefore, the masculine ego is afraid of facing Tao's demand of *coincidentia oppositorum*. This fear or threat is described by C.A.Meier in the words of the Rain Maker: "When I came to this district, I immediately realized that it was frighteningly out of Tao, whereby being here myself, I naturally was also out of Tao." For the Rain Maker, being "out of Tao" must have meant the total denial of his existence and universe. It must have made him unspeakably afraid so that he was driven to restore the lost Tao. Thus, the Rain Maker says: "All I could do, therefore, was to retire into wilderness (nature) and meditate, so as to get myself back." As Meier points out, this task of the Rain Maker to "put himself back in Tao again" must have been "hard work." Nevertheless, it had to be done; for, being "out of Tao" is "being out of cosmos," be it macrocosm or microcosm.

Not only getting back into Tao again, but also getting in touch with Tao is hard work. This is demonstrated by the old gardener practicing the Arts of Mr. Hun Tun. He is quite aware of the danger of *homo faber's* manipulating masculine ego, whose hubris may transform man into a heartless machine. The behavior of both the Rain Maker and the old gardener–one retires into the wilderness to meditate and the other works hard in the wilderness–may suggest to modern man a way to search for the soul. If we are not to destroy ourselves as a result of the inhuman operation of the technocratic machine, we must cultivate the feminine functioning of the ego so as to let the Tao, or Self, take its course. It is understandable that the seemingly unrelated images of the dog driving in New York and the gardener in ancient China kept coming to me as I read C.A. Meier's article, for they can be taken as amplificatory to the theme "Wilderness and the Search for the Soul of Modern Man," which Professor Meier elucidates with such profound insight.

NOTES

1. Chuang Tzu, *The Complete Works of Chuang Tzu*, trans. Burton Watson. New York: Columbia University Press, 1968, pp. 134-136.
2. C.A. Meier, this volume, p. 6.
3. C.G. Jung, *Psychological Types* (*Collected Works 6*). Princeton: Princeton University Press, 1971, pp. 457-458.
4. C.A. Meier, this volume p. 2.
5. Robert Lifton quoted by Beverly Beyette, "Harnessing a Healing Art in the Battle Against Violence," *Los Angeles Times*, Sept. 26, 1984, Part V.
6. Sam Keen, *Apology for Wonder*. New York: Harper and Row, 1969, p. 118.
7. C.G. Jung, "Commentary on 'The Secret of the Golden Flower,'" *Alchemical Studies* (*Collected Works 13*). Princeton: Princeton University Press, 1967, pp. 15-16.
8. *The I Ching*, trans. Richard Wilhelm. Princeton: Princeton University Press, 1967, p. 297.
9. *I Ching: Book of Changes*, trans. James Legge. New York: Bantam Books, 1964, p. 355.
10. *Chuang Tzu: Taoist Philosopher and Chinese Mystic*, trans. Herbert A. Giles. London: George Allen and Unwin, Ltd., 1961, p. 125.
11. Ibid. (The same page as the preceding note.)
12. *A Source Book in Chinese Philosophy*, trans. and comp. Wing-tsit Chan. Princeton: Princeton University Press, 1963, p. 266.
13. *The Complete Works of Chuang Tzu*, trans. Burton Watson, p. 58.
14. Ibid, p. 97.

15. Marie-Louise von Franz, *Patterns of Creativity Mirrored in Creation Myths*. Zurich: Spring Publication, 1972, p. 93.
16. C.G. Jung, "Epilogue to 'Essays on Contempory Events,'" *Civilization in Transition (Collected Works 10)*. Princeton: Princeton University Press, 1964, p. 242.
17. Barbara Hannah, *Jung, His Life and Work*. New York: G.P. Putnam's Sons, 1976, p. 129.
18. See footnote 7 above.

Joseph L. Henderson

3 *The Four Eagle Feathers*

After reading "Wilderness and the Search for the Soul of
Modern Man" I asked myself, as others must have done,
what contribution I have made to the process of harmonizing the macrocosm with the microcosm—a task that
the ancients understood and came to regard as one that
could not be left to the gods but belonged to humans to
accomplish. I have no doubt that my friend Fredy Meier
rightly understands and applies his knowledge in order
to connect his response to nature with the archetypal
aspect of the unconscious. With regard to myself I am
not so sure. I have tried to do my duty to "nature." Over
the years I have given a few dollars to the Sierra Club,
The Wilderness Society, The Wildlife Society and The
Audubon Society, and I have responded actively to re-
quests to save whales, seals, otters, redwoods and the
San Francisco Bay. I also enjoy my garden and feel
very protective of the undeveloped wooded canyon bordering my property; but none of these efforts or responses
does very much for the "soul," as I feel it.

It suddenly came to me that much of my response to

nature lies concealed in dream books I had kept while
in analysis with Jung many years ago in Zürich. One of
these dreams I still remember vividly. In it, I saw a series
of mountain ranges each one higher than the next, rising
from the sagebrush desert of Nevada near the town
where I was born. There is, in fact, a beautiful range of
snowy peaks which I saw every day from our house
during my childhood. I often explored those peaks during
the summers we spent on the working ranch we owned,
which was situated on the foothills of this range. Once
in early adolescence, I had a rather frightening experience
when looking toward the mountains: I thought I saw
the winding road we traveled to the ranch turning to
water or some fluid substance. I felt immediately, even
at that early age, the impermanence of all sentient im-
pressions and the precious need we have to keep a firm
foothold on life. I quickly stopped my psychedelic fantasy and returned to so-called normal consciousness.

The mountain ranges in my dream were not at all
like those real mountains, nor like any other mountains
I have ever seen, but I felt them to be in some way similar. Moreoever, there was a remarkable symbolic element
that emerged from the far side of each of these ranges:
a round object surmounted by a vertical eagle's feather.
Altogether, there were four ranges and four eagle feathers. The whole scene with its symmetrical arrangement
of symbols did not seem strange or in any way frightening. The image gave me the sense that the outer world
of nature, the macrocosm, is not alien, but akin to our
own unique inner vision. The symbol makes the bridge
between them.

There is an eloquent statement by Mircea Eliade
about this function of the symbol which I would

like to quote:

A religious symbol translates a human situation into cosmological terms and vice versa. Man does not feel himself isolated in the Cosmos; he is open to the World which, thanks to the symbol, becomes 'familiar.' On the other hand the cosmological meaning of such symbolism allows him to escape from a subjective situation and to recognize the objectivity of his personal experiences.[1]

In my case, the dream of the mountain ranges was "familiar" because of my early experience of real mountains, but the symbol created something which seemed to transform the cosmos into a device which informed me of many things as yet beyond my grasp.

The round object later came to mean an earth-bound sense of wholeness and unity, whereas the eagle feather represented a magic flight into regions of higher consciousness. Together they generated a promise that these need not be polar opposites, but complementary opposites unified as only a symbolic representation can accomplish. Remembering my early fantasy in which the ground of Being, the road toward the mountains, gave way and threatened to plunge me into a psychotic state, I learned to recognize the healing property of this later symbol. The number four, marking the number of mountain ranges and their symbols, came to mean a great deal to me in future years. I felt it to be a significant reference to the archetype of initiation, and it was the impetus for a lifelong study culminating in a book, *Thresholds of Initiation*,[2] and numerous lectures on that subject. The symbol of the eagle feather suggested an American Indian influence and thus anticipated another absorbing interest of mine, the study of Indian cultures from a psychological point of view.

In reviewing this stage of inner exploration, I now see how such an awakening of inner activity is likely to become prophetic in its anticipation of future actions in the world. Is this what harmonizing the microcosm with the macrocosm means? If so, I think we have to revise our sense of time. Time in the rational scheme of things is neatly divided into past, present and future. This may logically be necessary for many reasons such as making calendars, clocks, and weather reports, but it fails to account for the data of experience that Jung called synchronicity–data that unify subjective and objective states of being at the same time. Time in the popular sense seems also to include space. We even speak of a space of time. In this way of thinking, are we not again limited to past, present and future as an artificial linear progression which can never really be perceived, but only conceptualized?

The American artist Morris Graves was fond of drawing what he called *spirit birds* which had extraordinary eyes, and he painted their spacial ambience which he called *space of consciousness*. In doing this he brought together macro- and microcosm into a space that seemed both personal and timeless. It suggests to me Jung's idea of synchronicity, where objective and subjective states of being coincide. Psychologically, we may be justified in calling them timeless even when there seems to be some sort of serial process at work.

The dream image of the mountains and their symbols which I described earlier, caused me to awaken to a cultural task that resulted in a study of initiation in later years. Although the dream did not reveal this overtly, I made the connection only in retrospect. It would be more correct to say that my dream expressed something that was already true both in its literal and symbolic context and only awaited further concretization. I might not have brought it into reality at all but merely kept it as an image. I am reminded of A.E., the Irish poet who said, "keep in your soul some images of magnificence...." Might this not be enough?

Nonetheless, I would never have understood my dream if I had not had to bring it into reality, and I had no notion of how this could be done until it was done. Thus there seems to be a kind of synchronicity in which time forms a continuum or link between conception and delivery, a link that may span a period of many years. Previous knowledge of this first came to me after a particularly meaningful visit with Jung in the 1950's, long after he had ceased to see me as an analysand. This was the period I like to think of as his time for telling stories. He loved to tell them even if, sometimes to one's exasperation, they took too much time from one's precious analytical hour.

On this occasion Jung told me of an experience which he said had shown him that the interpretation of a dream or vision may not be possible until some future event has occurred. When alone at Bollingen, he had an impression that he thought must have been a dream when he heard soft footsteps going around the tower and then voices laughing and talking. When he went to the window there was nothing to see. This happened twice and the second time he had the visual image of peasant boys in their Sunday clothes who had come down from the mountains in a long procession. This dream and Jung's waking impression have been related in *Memories, Dreams and Reflections*. I will not repeat it here except to say how many years after his dream or vision, he tells us that he read a seventeenth century chronicle by Renward Cysat, who tells the following story: "On a high pasture of Mount Pilatus, which is particularly notorious for spooks–it is said that Wotan to this day practices his magic arts there–Cysat, while climbing the mountain, was disturbed one night by a procession of men who poured past his hut on both sides playing and singing– precisely what I had experienced at the Tower."[3]

Jung says he was not satisfied with a purely psychological interpretation of his experience, such as, that it merely meant that outward emptiness and silence are imaginatively "compensated by the image of a crowd of people."[4] Or was it merely a phenomenon of haunting, he asked himself? But this explanation did not ring true either. The interpretation of his dream and/or vision came to him when he found:

There actually existed, as I discovered, a real parallel to my experience. In the Middle Ages just such gathering of young men took place…In Italy they served as soldiers, [mercenaries] fighting for foreign princes. My vision, therefore, might have been one of these gatherings which took place regularly each spring when the young men, with singing and jollity, bade farewell to their native land.[5]

And so Jung concludes:

It would seem most likely to have been a synchronistic phenomenon. Such phenomena demonstrate that premonitions or visions very often have some correspondence in external reality.[6]

Following my earlier train of thought, I have been interested in the time sequences of this story, which span a period of many years, even centuries, from the late Middle Ages to the seventeenth century account of Cysat, thence to Jung's experience and finally his discovery of this account many years later. Therefore the synchronicity exists on so many levels that it suggests an occurrence outside time altogether, unless we consider this kind of *time* to have an archetypal meaning that transcends history.

Can we dispense with psychology entirely as Jung seems to be willing to do in this story? Could the fact that it was Jung and not someone else who had this experience have some specific meaning? I cannot help recalling what a joyous, youthful spirit he had at times and it seemed to increase during his mature years in his late forties and fifties. The serious student and son of a pastor of the Swiss Reform Church must have had many inhibitions to overcome before he could affirm fully the pleasure principle as he ultimately did. He told me once that in his student years he was usually the father-figure, the *senex* in any group of young people. Was there something in his own development that required a late blooming of the youthful *puer aeternus*—a movement in his psyche that activated the memory of a historical version of this archetype on a collective level of psychic awareness? I myself can only pose these questions, and so I leave the answer to psychological speculation. When writing this paper, I had a dream that Jung was alone at the bottom of a hill, standing there quietly. I went down to him and wondered what I should say to him. Should I say something reverential, or knowledgeable, something worthy of his genius as a thinker? Instead, I put my arm in his and said, "You gave us all such true enjoyment in your company with your 'festivity.'" He responded positively and we walked up the hill arm in arm. Even in the dream, I realized this was no ordinary idea of festivity but something informal, basic and spontaneous which created its own ritual. Did Wotan's magic high upon Mt. Pilatus on a spring evening conjure up a performance of the youthful dead, who must in death remain eternally young and be ready to enliven those who have come down from the mountains voluntarily and in consciousness of death as a new adventure of the human spirit?

As a result of Jung's story, I felt I better understood the nature of time sequences in my own life and their prophetic announcements in my dream material, and that I need not be unduly surprised or alarmed or incredulous at their appearance.

NOTES

1. Mircea Eliade, *Mephistopheles and the Androgyne: Studies in Religious Myth and Symbol*. New York: Sheed and Ward, 1965, p.207.
2. Joseph L. Henderson, *Thresholds of Initiation*. New York: Sheed and Ward, 1965.
3. C.G. Jung, *Memories, Dreams and Reflections*. New York: Vintage Books, 1965, p.230.
4. Ibid, p.231.
5. Ibid.
6. Ibid.

Laurens van der Post

4   *Wilderness — A Way of Truth*[1]

*For the hunter it is enough to grasp in outworn
fingers one feather of the white bird of truth
and die content.*   HEART OF THE HUNTER

One of the things that emerged at the Third World
Wilderness Congress was the feeling that we should be
more political and scientific, and that perhaps we are too
poetic and idyllic about wilderness. I am reminded of
something Jung said to me not long before he died. He
said that the truth needs scientific expression; it needs
religious expression and artistic expression. It needs the
poet and the musician. And even then, he said, you
only express a part of it.

The truth is total, and the inspirational idea that falls
into the human consciousness is total. It is the artist in
us who is able to apprehend the original inspiration in its
totality. But we are condemned by the nature of consciousness, according to our own particular gifts, to serve
and express it only in part.

While both the political and scientific approaches are
vitally necessary, it is important also to remember that
they work well only if they serve a transcendent vision.
Since the French Revolution we have lived in a time
when people increasingly think all the answers to life

are political ones. But while the political approach can carry out a vision, it cannot create one. The vision has to come from somewhere else. There can be a political vision of how to serve the wider plan of life, and the best politicians have it, but the values must come from somewhere else. Politics cannot create its own values.

However, the political approach is tremendously important. People who have a gift for politics perform an enormous service and one for which there is often very little gratitude, because we project all the failures onto them. A nation which does not take its politics seriously is doomed. In Asia, for instance, marvelous spiritually orientated cultures and civilisations have in a sense failed themselves because they didn't take the political approach sufficiently seriously. They never developed political systems for expressing the spiritual values. One of the great saving graces of the Western world, from the time of the Greeks, is that we have taken very seriously this problem of expressing values in an organised manner. In one of the great moments in Dante's *Divine Comedy*, written in the Middle Ages, he is asked whether life would not have been better if there had been no citizens—which means cities, for citizens live in cities. And he said that the answer was without a doubt no, it would not be better. Life needs citizens; it needs the political approach, too. But the political aspect is only a very small part of the total picture. It does not create the original values. Political systems work well only if they serve a transcendent, apolitical vision.

The difference between politics and this great apolitical vision is like the difference between true science and applied science. Applied science doesn't necessarily serve the progression of science. Einstein said that his great concept of the universe, the theory of relativity, came to him in less time than it takes to clap your hands, but it took a lifetime to prove it. The vision which his science served was greater than the merely scientific vision.

Some of our scientists talk about "managing wilderness," and this worries me a bit. It is like saying they want to control revelation. But the moment you try to control it, there is no revelation. Not one of those scientists could have created the vision of something like wilderness. The vision of wilderness is not very complicated. We try to give it elaborate definitions, but we all know what wilderness really is, because we have it inside ourselves. We know it is a world in which every bit of nature counts and is important to us, and we know when it is not there. Every person in the modern world knows how deprived they are in this area.

Those of us who have spent time in the wilderness are aware of the fact that there is something more to wilderness than we ourselves can express. This is rooted perhaps in the effect that wilderness has on human beings who have become estranged from nature, who live in industrialised environments and are therefore estranged in a sense from their natural selves. Wilderness has a profound impact on them, as well as on those of us more familiar with it.

I can perhaps illustrate this best by the example of three boys of different families and different nationalities, whose parents regarded them as "problem sons." All three boys had very privileged backgrounds, but somehow they could not come to terms with their own environments and with their own futures. Their parents came to me and asked what they could do to help their sons, because schools, doctors and educationalists did not seem to help. And I found a strange aboriginal voice in me saying, "Send them to the wilderness." I persuaded their parents to send them out to Zululand where they went on a wilderness trail with Ian Player. Nothing was said to them about themselves. All they had was the mirror which nature presented to them, and through this experience, which had a profound psychological impact on them, they found something of themselves and the wilderness within. They returned to Europe and to their schools and universities, and today all three are creative citizens distinguishing themselves in the world.

Wilderness is an instrument for enabling us to recover our lost capacity for religious experience. The religious area is far more than just the Church. If you look at the history of Europe since Christ, you will see that the Church has tended to be caught up in the social problems of its time, just as it is today, and to be less than the religion it serves. The churches and great cathedrals are really, in the time scale of human history, just tents on the journey somewhere else.

What wilderness does is present us with a blueprint, as it were, of what creation was about in the beginning, when all the plants and trees and animals were magnetic, fresh from the hands of whatever created them. This blueprint is still there, and those of us who see it find an incredible nostalgia rising in us, an impulse to return and discover it again. It is as if we are obeying that one great voice which resounds and resounds through the *Upanishads* of India: "Oh man, remember." Through wilderness we remember, and are brought home again.

When we contemplate the future of wilderness today, we see it as a place without human beings, where people go only as visitors. But we forget that there was once such a person as the "wilderness man." The original wilderness contained not only plants and trees and animals, but also people.

When we talk about primitive people in the world today, we are not really talking about them in the sense of *first* people. Most of our ideas of primitive people are based on what we have observed of great indigenous cultures which are already well advanced on the way to civilisation. The American Indians, for instance, were far more in communion with their instincts than we are, but they were by no means primitive. They were already very sophisticated. Peoples like the Navajo and Hopi had their own forms of civilisation. The Navajo were great sheep people, while the agricultural Hopi went in for husbandry. They had already crossed the great divide and tamed a part of nature for their own uses. The great black societies of Africa are also peoples of very vast and sophisticated forms of human organisation.

But Africa did produce a first person. And this first person has haunted my life from the time I was born, because I had a nurse who was one of the last survivors in my part of Africa of the first people. I owe her a tremendous amount, because through her the private person in me, the child in me, took wing.

In later life, I had the privilege for about three and a half years to be in constant contact with these first people of Africa, the Bushmen. When we contemplate them I think we realise the horror of what we have done— that in destroying wilderness we have destroyed "wilderness man." In a way, that is the greatest loss of all, because this person could have been our real bridge to knowing wilderness and nature in the way in which it is known by the Creator and in which it should really be known.

I would like to tell you a little about these people. It is not a romantic vision because, obviously, they had their faults too, and they were very human faults. But they were faults, in so far as I could observe them, that had no unnecessary complications to them. They were faults that were in proportion and that were incorporated and kept in position by the great necessities of nature, by the totality of their way of life. They committed themselves to nature as a fish to the sea, and nature was kinder to them by far than any civilisation ever was.

The one outstanding characteristic of these people as I knew them, and which distinguished them from us, was that wherever they went, they felt they were known. The staggering loss of identity and meaning that we in the modern world experience was unknown to them. As St. Paul says, "Then shall I know as even now I am known." This sense of being known has completely abandoned us in the modern world, because we have destroyed the wilderness persons in ourselves and banished the wilderness that sustained them from our lives. And because of the absence of a wilderness person in ourselves, we are left with a kind of loneliness, an inadequate comprehension of what life can be. We have become the greatest collection of human know-alls that life has ever seen. But the feeling that our knowing is contained in a greater form of being known has gone.

One of the most extraordinary things to me about these first people was their lack of aggression. I asked them if they had ever had war, and they said, oh yes, they had fought and were known as very great fighters. Except for when they fought against the Black and the White people, they had had only one war among themselves. I asked, "Was it an awful war?" And they said, "It was a terrible war." I asked, "Were many people killed?" And they said, "One man was killed." That was enough. One man. It didn't have to be numbers. In this terrible world in which we live today, we think things only matter if we know them in numbers. We talk about the sum of human misery. There is no such thing in the wilderness. The sum of human misery is really an abstraction, because misery is never more than what one person can feel. It is inflicted on one person at a time. This misery was enough for them. And I asked, "What did you do?" They said, "Well, we decided that those of us who had done the killing should never meet again because we were not fit to meet one another."

So they drew a line across the desert. And for centuries they had not crossed the line, in case they should take life again. They held the life of one person to be so precious. I asked them, "But how can you draw a line in the desert?"–because one side of it looked to me very much like the other. They always thought that I was singularly stupid and uneducated, and, of course, I am, in their terms. I was a baby, not even in the kindergarten class. And they said, "Well, you see, no two dunes are alike, no two plants are alike. It is part of our education to know what dunes and what plants are the dividing lines, and we never cross those dividing lines."

There went a people to whom life was full of meaning. They always moved in small companies, and the groups I knew best never exceeded twenty-three in number. That was the entire community, and everyone was a clear-cut individual with individual gifts, making indi-

vidual contributions to their little society. There was
none of the smearing and blurring of personality that we
get in the mass societies of the West and of Asia. Yet to
them, everything was family. They had no captains or
kings, and the highest title they could bestow was to call
someone a grandfather or grandmother. The stars were
part of the family too. The star Sirius, for instance, the
great dog star, was grandmother Sirius to whom they
prayed. They would say, "Oh grandmother Sirius, who
sits there with a heart of plenty and so full of light, give
us who do not have so much, some of your plenty."
And they believed it happened and it helped. The whole
of the cosmos was a family. They had an extraordinary
feeling of kinship that burnt like a flame and kept them
on course, that kept them warm and full of meaning.
I have seen a woman at night hold her little boy up to
the stars. I asked, "Why the stars?" And they said,
"Don't you know the stars are great hunters there in the
outer dark? She is asking the stars to take from her son
the heart of a little child and give him the heart of a star
instead."

The sense of communion that these people had with
the cosmos came out above all in their stories. There was
nothing about which they did not have a story. There
is one story that I want to tell you, because I think it
sums up the importance of serving the truth, even if one
has only a part of the truth which one can fulfill in one's
own lifetime.

This is a story of a hunter. The people in the groups
I knew all hunted, but there was always one man who
was better at it than most. Often he also happened to be
the musician. They had musical instruments shaped like
a bow and the hunter who shot so well with his bow

was often the one who also played beautifully on this wonderful bow-stringed instrument.

The story goes that one day this hunter was out hunting and became very thirsty. He came to the edge of a pool—it was in the rainy season—and bent down to drink some of the water. And as he looked into this pool which was deep blue with the midnight blue of an African summer sky, he suddenly saw in the rippling mirror below him the reflection of a great white bird. He looked up quickly, startled, but the bird had already gone. From that moment on, he wasn't the same. He lost all interest in hunting. The people, because they loved him, tried desperately to revive his desire of hunting, but it had totally abandoned him. One day he said to his people, "I am sorry; I am going. I am going to find this bird whose reflection I saw. I have got to find it." And he said goodbye and vanished.

The story goes that he went all over Africa, all over what they then naturally thought of as the entire world. And whenever he came to places where there were people, he would describe the bird to them and ask if they had seen it, and they would say, "What a pity you didn't come last night, because the bird was roosting nearby." So it went on and on until, toward the end of his days when he was quite an old man, he came to an enormous mountain right in the heart of Africa. He asked the people at the foot of the mountain if they knew anything about this bird. And they said, oh yes, it came to roost every night on top of the mountain. So he climbed the mountain and when he came close to the top, he found the summit was a sheer cliff which he couldn't scale. His strength was worn out and he knew he could go no further. He stood there looking into the red and scarlet sunset of Africa and thought, "I shall never see this white bird whose reflection is all I know." And he prepared himself to lie down to die.

Then at that moment, a voice inside him said, "Look!" He looked up and, in the dying light of the African sunset, he saw a white feather floating down from the mountain top. He held out his hand and the feather came into it, and grasping the feather, he died.

When the Bushmen told me this story, I asked, "What sort of bird was this?" And they said, "The bird has many names, but we think of it as the Great White Bird of Truth."

Here we have an example of the instinctive symbolism of people who are spiritually "aware." The imagery comes naturally out of their being, putting them on the trail of truth, yet with a humility that does not try to grasp it all at once. Some of us would like the whole of our wilderness dream at once. We are impatient, and feel if we don't get it immediately, we shall never see it. But in this story just the reflection of the bird, not even the bird itself, was enough to send a man on its trail—and one feather from that bird made his life worthwhile and allowed him to die content.

The processes of history work slowly. There are no short cuts in creation. Things happen by the planting and sowing of seeds, and do not appear all at once. We must have the humility of spirit to recognise how small, in a sense, is the success we can achieve in a single lifetime. We cannot do it all. But what we can do is set things in their right direction, and I think that is beginning to happen. As we do that, since life is universal and we do not control it, something far greater than ourselves begins to work. This puts at our disposal, late as the hour is, time enough for the right things to happen. There is always time enough, no matter how desperate the situation, for the complete thing to happen.

I would like all of us who are pursuing wilderness to take this in, and to know that if we follow in the way of the "wilderness man," we too shall grasp a feather of truth. And that one day, one day that indeed will come, we shall be able to contemplate the whole bird in its entirety.

I would like you to reach out and believe this. I would like to make a pact with you that our wilderness dream will come true. The Earth today is wounded and sore. But our pursuit of the wilderness dream will bring about not only the protection of the wilderness such as we have it today, but also the rehabilitation of the Earth, with people able to live in the wilderness state of communion with it, following the White Bird of Truth.

This will come. Nothing can stop it, for nothing can stop a dream that is true. If you go back into the history of humankind, you find that in all the great cultures–the Greek, the Babylonian, the Chinese, the Japanese and our own–everything begins with a dream. Think of the dreams in our own Bible–of the tremendous dream of Jacob's Ladder, for example. Think of the dream which started the great Greek Homeric saga of the *Iliad* and the *Odyssey*, when a god sent a dream into the head of sleeping Agamemnon as he lay by the black ships on the great plain of Troy. It all starts with a dream. Until we can say at last, "Pass, world. I am the dreamer that remains clear-cut against the sky." That is a quotation from a poem by a friend of mine.

We cannot, today, recreate the original "wilderness man" in shape, form and habitat. But we can recover him, because he exists in us. He is the foundation in spirit or psyche on which we build, and we are not complete until we have recovered him. Life not only involves being conscious of the moment in which we live, but also involves a vision of the future. And before we can live properly, before we can face the future, we have got to re-member. We have got to remember the needs and hunger of our instinctive, intuitive, natural self. It needs our consciousness, because without our consciousness it has no life. But without its prompting, our life has no mean-ing. In the modern world, we have become so engaged in *doing* that we have become divorced from the aspect of ourselves which gives us being.

The real task of every generation is first to make what is new and contemporary. The first people, the wilder-ness people, were not complete. They needed something more which they were in search of, and there was an enormous act of evolution that had to occur. But in the lopsided way in which the so-called civilising process takes place, one part that was glaringly lacking was pulled out of the wholeness and developed to the exclusion of others. In the process of developing it, we fell into the heresy of thinking that that was the lot, and of course it isn't. What we need to do now, in very simple mathe-matical terms is to make the first the last, and to bring what was left behind up to where we are. We still carry around with us the world of nature within. We need to match that to the world without, to make the world with-out more and more an expression of the world within.

The reason we exploit, damage and savage the Earth is because we are out of balance. We have lost our sense of proportion. And we cannot be proportionate unless we honour the wilderness and the natural person without ourselves. That is where the balance comes from. Our greed and aggression and corruption by power comes from cheating that first person within ourselves out of his natural inheritance, as Jacob cheated Esau. The whole great progression of evolution as represented in the Bible is based on a monstrous act of deception which passed for intelligence. It is a form of intelligence and has to be seen symbolically, and I do not want to suggest that that development is invalid. It *is* valid, but we should recognise that it is not the whole story. Somewhere, beyond the walls of our awareness, the Esau side, the wilderness side, the hunter side, the seeking side of ourselves, is waiting to return.

NOTES

1. This article originally appeared in *Wilderness: The Way Ahead*, Vance Martin and Mary Inglis, eds. The Findhorn Press, Scotland and The Lorian Press, Wisconsin, 1984.

Ian Player

5 Ndumu to Inverness: the Story of a Personal Journey

In October 1983 I sat in the audience of delegates to the Third World Wilderness Congress and listened intently to the speech of Professor C.A.Meier. Outside the hall, the first winds of autumn were blowing through the streets of Inverness and leaves fell into the dark and swift flowing river. It was fitting that the congress should be held in Scotland, a Celtic stronghold, because so many wilderness areas in the world were protected and administered by those of Celtic descent.

The day was extraordinarily special for me because C.A.Meier's speech dealt with subjects that had come to concern me deeply. I had been involved with the outer wilderness for thirty-three years and in the past five years had had a glimpse of the inner. My journey to Inverness had been much longer than the air flight from Durban to London and the continuing train journey to Scotland. The journey had begun twenty-nine years ago and in many ways was most improbable. Space prevents me from presenting a detailed account of it, but I hope that I can convey the essence of how important this journey has been for me, and how indebted I am to those who carry on the work of C.G. Jung, particularly his close collaborator C.A. Meier, whose work on psychology and religion has answered many questions for me.

The story begins in 1954 when, as a young game ranger, I was stationed at a game reserve called Ndumu on the northernmost boundary of Zululand adjoining Mozambique. I had completed two intensive years with the Natal Parks Game and Fish Preservation Board and had been promoted to a senior ranger. In those two years I had served in many of the game reserves of Zululand: at Richards Bay, then a tiny village on the Indian Ocean and now a huge port; at Lake St. Lucia, which was sixty-four kilometres long, with an abundance of hippo, crocodile, flamingo and pelican, sea fish and fresh water fish, and the highest forest covered sand dunes in the world; at Hluhluwe game reserve, the home of the last surviving black rhinoceros in Southern Africa, and at Umfolozi game reserve, where the white rhino survived and were slowly increasing. In those two years, I had learned a lot about human beings and about wildlife. I had been law enforcement officer, public relations man, sanitary inspector, bait capture officer, tourist guide and vehicle repair man. There had not been a dull moment. For the first time in my life I felt fully involved.

I had left school at 17 and gone to the Second World War with the South African Army, and had served in Italy at the tail end of the war. That too was an experience I would not have missed, but it had disrupted my life, and I returned home in 1946 feeling lost and disturbed, unable to settle down. For six years I wandered about Southern Africa. For a while I was an apprentice gold miner, working two thousand metres below the surface. I became a prospector, and later a farm hand, in Zimbabwe. On the coast, I caught fish with rod and line to earn my living, then moved inland to work in a factory. It was only when I started working in wild country that my sense of equilibrium began to return. I had the good fortune to meet an old Zulu, Magqubu Ntombela, at Umfolozi game reserve and he became initially my guide, teacher, and companion, and then years later, one of my most important friends. I am deeply indebted to him, this most natural and whole man.

At Ndumu, my work took me to many wild sections of the game reserve. I walked with Zulu game guards, learning the names of plants, birds, insects, trees and animals. I canoed down the Usutu and Pongolo rivers, counting hippo and crocodile, learning their habits and seeing and beginning to understand their role in nature. It was a meeting point for many southern and northern species of birds, and I learned to differentiate between the bird calls and grew to understand the nocturnal and diurnal rhythms. There were unhappy and miserable days too, when we had to arrest people for offences against the game laws. This meant long journeys to the nearest court and a weary wait for our cases to be called. I questioned the validity of taking tribal people into custody for acts that to them were perfectly normal, in fact part of their way of life. They lived in a different stream of life from ourselves and I frequently felt that we were going upstream against the current. I voiced my doubts, and on occasion this put me at odds with local officialdom.

There were the good days spent in the bush, camping out near kraals of the amáTonga tribe and helping them to keep the hippo and elephant from the fields of maize, cassava and sorghum. At night they played their drums and other instruments, and danced around the fire until the early hours of the morning. There was unhappiness here though, from drunkenness. They made a liquor from the marula fruit (*Sclerocarya caffra*) which they collected and allowed to ferment. Women with young children strapped to their backs would drink until they could no longer stand for drunkenness. Many babies were burnt and scarred for life when their mothers tripped over pots of boiling water, or fell into the fire. Deep down I had the feeling that this was a reaction to the force of western technology that had disrupted their lives. We had interrupted their story and they were looking for ways to adapt. Some of them could not do it, and like so many aboriginal people in the world, they took to liquor. It was the one certain, if temporary, escape. I was later to see this in the aboriginal people on the west coast of Australia, and the Amerindians in North America.

The amaTonga people of northeastern Zululand were very much a part of the natural world and there was a symbiotic relationship between them and the neighbouring wild creatures. Abandoned fields became grazing places for antelope, hippo, and elephant, and spilt grain was food for seed-eating birds. They had an inherent understanding of the rhythm of the land and a pattern of survival was deeply imprinted within them. They made use of all the wild fruits, and after the floods had receded, they lightly ploughed the alluvial soil in the lakes that adjoined the two rivers. But great changes were taking place with the introduction of modern medicines, the decline in infant mortality, increasing mechanisation and the elimination of malarial outbreaks.

The population was growing and the people were suffering in a long, slow and painful way, because they were not really conscious of what was taking place. The hospitals manned by missionaries were magnificent, equal to any in the world. There was much alleviation of pain and physical suffering. The government anti-malarial inspectors were dedicated men, and they worked tirelessly to wipe out this ancient decimator of human beings. But in my heart, I knew that we who had brought technology had not considered the consequences. On the one hand, we had brought help, but on the other, the help was destroying the fabric of their society. I appreciated that the amaTonga and I were, individually and collectively, part of the historical process, but I felt that the European influence was not taking this historical process into account. It was a dreadful dilemma because the land was being devastated too, and could not hold the increasing number of people. Always it was the children who suffered first. Much of what I write now was an unconscious questioning, but it was confirmed for me when I read what Lord Bryce had to say, in 1921:
Do not give to a people institutions for which it is unripe in the simple faith that the tool will give skill to the workman's hand. Respect facts. Man is in each country not what we wish him to be, but what Nature and History have made him.

My work was to protect the Ndumu game reserve, a 25,000 acre area rich in diversity. The reserve had been proclaimed in 1927, but was neglected until 1952, when the first resident ranger had been appointed. I had to fence the reserve, make the roads, and ensure that there was no destruction of game, trees, plants or birds. Many of the amaTonga tribespeople lived in the game reserve, but any infringement of the game laws meant that they had to leave. There were terrible divisions between those game guards who were tribesmen, and their neighbours. But, the people of Africa are so forgiving that there were times when I was ashamed at our culture's insensitivity. I was wounded, too, by seeing people having to move from ancestral lands; however, it was necessary because this was the only way to protect this tiny remnant of once wild Africa. At the same time, I could see that there were many factors beyond my control or influence that were going to affect the game reserve in the years ahead. The building of dams and hotels and the inrush of tourism were going to change not only the landscape, but the soul of the tribespeople and those of us who worked in these once wild lands.

In long hours of paddling canoes down the rivers, or sitting and watching crocodiles feeding on shoals of fish in the late evening while fruit bats called from yellow fever trees, I worried about the future of all wild Africa and its vulnerability to what man called progress. There were many scientists writing excellent papers on different aspects of wildlife and conservation in Africa, yet there was something lacking. I felt that it needed a poet or a writer to express the call of wild Africa and its importance to mankind. I would sit at night under the acacia trees near my bungalow and listen to hippo grunting and the amaTonga tribal drums thudding in the distance and echoing in the riverine forests. There was a heavy scent from the yellow Ansellia orchids and the flowers of the fever tree. What I was seeing, smelling and hearing was the old Africa. It had me in its grip but no one had been able, for me, to write about its meaning. Nothing that I had read had touched my soul.

Then one morning I collected my mail at the local trading store and someone had sent me Laurens van der Post's *Venture to the Interior*.[2] I had read all my life but here was a book I could not put down. "This man knows what Africa is all about," I repeated to myself, as I read the book into the night by the light of a paraffin lamp. What Laurens had to say touched something in my soul. He knew the old Africa and what it could do for mankind. I never thought that I would ever meet him. He lived in Britain and I was on the border of Mozambique in northeast Zululand. I felt too shy to write and tell him how his book had affected me and thought that was the end of it. But fate had other plans.

Fifteen years later, during a wildlife conservation career that had enabled me to serve in every game reserve in Zululand, while climbing the ladder of promotion to chief game conservator, I had to go to Britain. If anyone had told me at the time that my meeting with Laurens van der Post would lead me to read the work of Jung, I would have thought he was mad. Seventeen years in the civil service had left their mark. I had been inwardly bruised when I resisted being put into the mould. My work had led me to understanding the value of African wilderness and what it could do to help mankind to become whole. I felt too that the time spent in wild country had touched something within me that set me apart, turned me into an outsider. It was only with people who had had the same experience in wilderness that I was able to converse on another level.

It was with all this turmoil inside me that I went to London with the strange assignment to sell surplus white rhino from the Umfolozi game reserve to open park zoos. I had hardly any idea of how to do it, let alone where to begin. Then Dr. T.C.Robertson, an old school friend of Laurens van der Post, gave me an introductory letter. He explained: "Laurens was in a P.O.W. camp in Java under the Japanese and everyone who is important in the world seems to have been in that camp. Go and see Laurens, he will understand about your rhino and your wilderness experiences. He knows about these things."

I remember arriving early and walking round the cold streets of Chelsea, so that I would ring his doorbell exactly at the appointed hour. Like so many others before me, I was immediately enveloped by this man with his blue eyes of infinite depth. We sat in his drawing room with the view of all London around us, yet the sense of Africa was so strong that it was as though we were around a fire in the bush. We talked at great length of our land, its beauties, problems, unhappiness and inspiration. I was very drawn to him and our friendship grew.

After I had been with the Natal Parks Board for twenty-two years, I left to become programme director of the International Wilderness Leadership Foundation. Since 1958 I had been involved in helping to educate people to understand the importance of having wilderness areas which were part of, but distinct from, game reserves. In South Africa it was a new concept, and a difficult one for people to accept.

In 1974, my work became broader in scope and I made arrangements for young people and adults from the United States, Europe and the United Kingdom to hike on wilderness trails in the wild areas of Zululand and the eastern Transvaal. Laurens van der Post himself came to South Africa to go on trail with Magqubu Ntombela and me. Sitting around the acacia wood fire with all the sounds of Africa in the night and talking to Laurens did much to open up perceptions of which I was only dimly aware. Magqubu, with his intuitive sensing, gave Laurens his Zulu name after only a few hours. He called him Nkunzimalanga—The one who pushes everything in front of him but so gently that no one is aware of it.

We had an interesting experience on this trail. Lions, black rhino, buffalo and other wild animals moved around near the camp at night. Bearing in mind that we slept on the ground in the open, and not in tents, we had to keep watch. There were so few of us that it would have meant long hours for each person. Then at about nine o'clock, two young white rhino bulls walked to us and lay down under a huge sycamore fig tree about ten metres from our fire. Magqubu said, "We can go to sleep, they will make sure we wake if lions, buffalo or black rhino come near us." And so it was. The white rhino is a gentle, non-aggressive animal unless it is really provoked. They slept until the early morning when they woke us with their snorting and shuffling, and we kept watch until dawn.

In 1976 Laurens sent me his book on Jung.³ I had read everything Laurens had written, but when I opened this book and saw that it was about a psychologist, I thought, "This is not for me." Long ago I had tried to read something of Freud's, and could not do so. So for the first time I put one of Laurens' books aside.

A year later, I was heavily involved in organising and planning the First World Wilderness Congress in Johannesburg. Once more, I turned to Laurens for help at critical moments when politics, human idleness and a host of other problems threatened to destroy the congress. Nkunzimalanga helped to ensure that what we had set about to do took place. The congress was an outstanding success. For the first time at a conservation congress in South Africa, there were black politicians, white politicians, tribal people, a Kalahari Bushman leader, bankers, poets, industrialists, writers, painters, and scientists, and speakers from all over the western world.

There was only one disappointment. Laurens had spoken of C. A. Meier. He had invited him to come, but Meier was unable to attend. Fate again had other plans.

In 1978, on the way to America from Johannesburg via London, I was in the middle of a crisis, low in spirit and wondering what was happening in my life. At Heathrow airport, I happened to see a paperback copy of Laurens' book on Jung. I remembered that he had sent me the hardback which I had not read. Instinctively I bought it and I read it on the seven hour journey across the Atlantic. I was stunned. The book I had put aside two years before had opened a new chapter in my life. Here was the answer to so much that had been troubling me. Here too, was the man Jung, who had explored and mapped the interior wilderness of man.

I phoned Laurens' flat but he was away and I spoke to Ingaret, his wife, who told me that she had once worked with Jung. Through a series of synchronistic events, slow in unfolding but essential in my development, I met the one and only Jungian analyst in Natal, Dr. Gloria Gearing. The hour she spared me each week became the most important part of my life.

I read everything I could about Jung and those who worked with him: C. A. Meier, Marie-Louise von Franz (oh, the revelation and the pain of *puer aeternus*), Barbara

Hannah and others in America–John Sanford, James Hillman, James Kirsch. I read until I was like a man who had been hungry, starving for food and then had eaten and eaten until not another morsel could be digested. The digestive process is continuing.

In 1980, the Second World Wilderness Congress was held, on the Barrier Reef of Australia, in the small town of Cairns. Of all the speeches of the week, the one by Laurens van der Post and his closing address moved the audience most. He spoke not only of the African wilderness and his experience in it, but also of the prisoner-of-war camp in Java and the wonderful behaviour of the Australians within the camp. He talked, also, of Jung, in simple direct terms so that the audience understood. It was a great contrast to some of the detailed scientific papers of those people who were looking through the keyhole to wilderness instead of through the wide open door.

In July 1983, I was on trail in the Umfolozi game reserve and camped on the Black Umfolozi river beneath one of the giant sycamore fig trees. My companions were Gloria Gearing, her husband, John Brouckaert, an American visitor, and Jane Bedford, who is married to Laurens van der Post's nephew, Tommy Bedford. Shortly before going on the trail, I had read an article entitled "Nature Awe," written by Jay Vest, an American. It made a deep impression and something stirred within.

Jay Vest wrote about how the ancient Celts had set aside and made pilgrimages to the nemetons, the great groves of trees, to experience the soul mood.He described how the Celts had suffered at the hands of imperial Christians who wanted to assimilate the sacred groves into church institutions. Vest says: "The church had to resort to threatening the people's immortal souls, as well as burning 'non-believers' at the stake in order to effect the desired change of worship."4

My mother was of direct Scottish descent and something of the Celtic relationship revived within me. This had helped to explain my sensitivity and concern for the plight of the amaTonga and what they were going through when I was at Ndumu. Had not my most ancient ancestors experienced all this at the hands of imperial Christianity? Their story had been interrupted as well, in the same way as we had broken the thread of the amaTonga story. It went far beyond racial terms of black men and white men, and what the latter might have been doing to the former. We were part of an expanding wave that had gathered and tumbled everything together, joining the good and the bad of religions and cultures. This was revealed in a dream which suddenly flowed through me as we sat near the fire listening to the night-jars calling, lions roaring downriver, hyena howling as they followed the hunting lions, and rhino bulls bellowing across the river.

I had dreamt of a Norman church and in the left hand wall an enormous gum tree (Eucalypt) was embedded. I walked into the church and remarked that the roof was all right, then came outside and said to myself, "If the tree falls down, the church will come down. If the church falls down, it will drag the tree down." The dream said to me that Christianity and the belief in Celtic wilderness are inseparable; they had only been wrongly interpreted. It was a healing dream. For fifty years, there had been an unconscious struggle within me, because my formal Christian upbringing brought inner demands to attend church. I wanted instead to be in wild country, but both demands left a strong feeling of guilt. The gum tree for me symbolised the wilderness, because it was an old tree of the ancient continent of Australia. The Norman church was the old church of my youth and the roof was sound. The tree and the church were inseparably linked. The dream was God's grace resolving my unconscious battle of half a century. It seemed appropriately synchronistic too, that a family relative of Laurens was present, because it was his book that had started me on the path. That the dream should occur when Gloria Gearing was present, confirmed all she had done for me. The dream has never left me, and it has become as important as a foundation is for a house. It lies there glowing in the mind, waiting to be developed, built upon and expanded.

In that same month of July, Laurens wrote to tell me that it was now definite that C.A.Meier would be talking at the Third World Wilderness Congress. There were people in the South African delegation who made the long journey to Scotland specifically to hear his talk. When he had spoken, I walked out into the chill October day with a forester friend of mine from South Africa, a man deeply steeped in the scientific method, and a great lover of wilderness. We were both moved by Meier's description of the wilderness within. The paper was a confirmation of my life's work in the outer sphere of wilderness and the importance of furthering the inner journey. I reflected on the experience of taking 1,000 people, in groups of no more than six, from all over the world into the wild country of Zululand, with Magqubu Ntombela.

I had witnessed the inter-linking of the inner and the outer wilderness. C.A.Meier's talk made me realise the extent to which the response of the trailists revealed their relationship to their own inner reality. There were some who came straight out of cities such as Johannesburg and New York into wild African country for the first time in their lives. Within a few days they were perfectly at ease and wanted to stay longer, although to begin with, the power of the unconscious predator was mirrored in their obsessive fear of lion, leopard and hyena, even when they had been assured there was no danger. For many, the first experience of keeping watch at the fire alone at night was an overwhelmingly frightening time. The strange sounds and the initial unfamiliarity were full of imagined terrors, but when the red dawn flooded the African sky, most of them realised that the source of their fear had little to do with physical danger. It was the concern with the wild animals inside themselves that caused their worry. I was able to demonstrate it by pointing out that while they were keeping watch, they had stared into the fire where there was no danger. The physical danger lay beyond the fire and that was the direction they should have been facing. It was interesting, too, that before going on trail, many people had dreams of lions, and on trail, the first question was inevitably about snakes.

And this brings the story to an end except to add that in 1984 I had the good fortune to take Dr. John Sanford, his wife Lynn, Joan Winchell and Katie Sanford on trail with my organisation, the Wilderness Leadership School. This was followed by a trail with Drs. Lee Roloff and Vera Bührmann. I pray it is the beginning of the Jungian analysts' trek into the wilderness of Southern Africa, for the wild lands have much to teach us all. South Africa is in a political wilderness too, shunned by the western world because it is part of their shadow. The complexity of tribes, races, creeds and colours that make up South Africa and the unconscious striving for wholeness is a most fertile field for the Jungian analyst. It is my firm belief that as the psychology of C.G. Jung becomes more understood in Southern Africa, we could better find ourselves, and the world will find us once more.

So a journey that began in the wilds and heat of north-eastern Zululand where the great Usutu and Pongolo rivers meet and spill over into lakes, matured on the banks of the Ness river, the surrounding hills glistening with newly fallen snow. The Zulus say that there is only one god, Nkulunkulu–He who is greater than greater. That night, when the stars of the Northern Hemisphere glimmered in an unusually clear sky and I could hear the calls of wading birds on the edge of the Moray Firth, I gave thanks.

NOTES

1. Lord Bryce quoted by The Hon. Mr. Justice Frank Broome in "The Individual and the Community," from *White Africans are also People*, Sarah Gertrude Millin, comp. Cape Town: Howard Timmins. 1966, p. 172.
2. Laurens van der Post, *Venture to the Interior*. London: Hogarth Press, 1952.
3. Laurens van der Post, *C.G. Jung and the Story of Our Time*. London: Hogarth Press, 1976.
4. Jay Vest, *Nature Awe: Celtic Views of Nature*. Montana: Western Wildlands, Spring 1983, p. 43.

M. Vera Bührmann

6   Nature, Psyche and a Healing Ceremony of the Xhosa

Writing as an analytical psychologist about my transcultural research work, against the background of my
deep concern about the conservation of nature and of
the psychic health of humanity, I am deeply aware of the
mystery of nature and of psyche. I will try to convey
some of the mystery of healing when both of these are
combined and honoured.

I would like therefore to look at how some aspects
of nature can assist modern man in his search for a soul.
To do this I am going to describe two of the Xhosa healing and training ceremonies–the River Ceremonies.
I will try to convey the mystery of these ceremonies
and attempt to illustrate the constellation of the inner
healer who resides in the soul and who guides the work
of the outer healer and his patients. Identification with
and inflation by the power of the inner healer is guarded
against by the profound respect which the Xhosa healer
feels for the ancestors and the macrocosm, i.e., nature.

No living ritual is meaningless; the efficacy is often
difficult to *understand*, but when one is an involved par-

ticipant, one can *experience* its power to transform and to make whole. The healing power of these rituals to a large extent remains a mystery, no matter how much we try to conceptualise it and to fit it into a mould of our own making. Heraclitus "observed the mysteries not only in the cultic sense as an outward action, but as a sacred rite enacted in the soul."[1]

To appreciate Xhosa ritual and ceremonies, it is necessary to understand some of their cosmology and cultural beliefs, especially as these pertain to health and ill-health in their widest ramifications. A constant equilibrium must be maintained between certain cosmic powers, especially between good and evil. For equilibrium contributes to well-being in all areas of living, and disequilibrium causes trouble, misfortune and ill-health. The concept of this subtle balance or harmony between the macrocosm and microcosm which permeates C.A. Meier's article in this volume, is also the foundation of Xhosa thinking.

A central theme in their belief system is the role of the ancestors, the "living dead," and the relationship between them and their living kin. For health, happiness and success in life, a good relationship with constant interaction and communication between them is necessary; harmony and equilibrium must be maintained. (At a psychological level this would apply to the ego and the unconscious.) If this breakdown and disequilibrium occurs, the result will be sickness, unhappiness and misfortune. The breakdown is due to the neglect of the customs which should be performed to ensure vitality and hence the help and protection of the ancestors against the forces of evil. Such neglect is seen as lack of respect for the ancestors, who then turn their backs on their kin.

I see ancestors as psychic complexes, some of them archetypal. To a large extent, they are projected onto the outside world of nature: animals, plants, and the elements such as water–especially rivers, fire, lightning and thunder, etc. If these are not honoured, it can be seen as lack of respect for the created world. Everything in nature is conceived of as having some innate power. Human beings naturally are also carriers of projections and of symbolic meaning, as is often seen in their dreams.

The Xhosa know two kinds of ancestors: first I will describe the family and clan-linked ones whom "we know by their faces" and whose presence is always felt around the homestead and who share in the everyday life of living kin. They have very human attributes, being able to feel pleased or annoyed, hungry, thirsty, hot or cold and can make their wishes known through dreams. They differ, however, from their living kin by virtue of their greater wisdom.

The others are the Ancestors of the River and the Ancestors of the Forest. They are "not known by their faces." They are powerful and awesome and live under the water and in the forest. On account of their numinosity, they cannot be approached or consulted without special precautions being taken.

Psychologically, I see the former as the personification of complexes of the personal and cultural unconscious, and the latter as presenting archetypes of the collective unconscious.

The primary aim of the river ceremonies is to consult the Ancestors of the River, and to get their opinion or advice about a specific individual ("index person") or situation. At times their active help is also asked for. Therefore, there are minor variations in the performance of these ceremonies, depending on the need and the circumstances. To the best of my knowledge, they are performed primarily for healing and training of candidates for the healing profession.

All ceremonies are performed at the home of the index person so as to permit maximal participation by his relatives and his ancestors.

I will confine myself to those ceremonies I know best, i.e., those which are used in the treatment of a neurosis and especially those used for the treatment of thwasa. Thwasa is an illness with predominantly mental features which is caused by the ancestors calling an individual to their service, i.e., for him to become a healer, a mediator between the living and the ancestors. Thwasa, in Western thinking, is an umbrella term for the neuroses in contrast to the psychoses. It is a mental state in which there is considerable psychic turmoil, and at times even chaos. It can be said that it is a state of "psychic wilderness" which is partly due to neglect of certain obligations and disrespect for psychic elements. It must be noted that there is no sharp distinction between treatment of sick people and the training to become healers, except in the final stages of training.

The River Ceremonies best demonstrate the non-separation of human beings from nature. They also illustrate the reverence for the powers that are innate to nature, the ways in which the healer uses and even manipulates these powers and the effectiveness of activating archetypes and their symbolic realisation. To me, the mystery of psyche and nature, and the effectiveness of their cooperation, become apparent in these ceremonies.

The first River Ceremony is the initial one to be performed in the treatment/training of an individual. It is only done after a preliminary period of treatment by dream analysis, milieu therapy, purification and intlombes (a ritual dance and singing performance). The final deciding factors, however, are the messages from the ancestors as conveyed in the dreams of the patient and the healer. From my observations, it seems that a certain degree of ego integration must be reached before this ceremony treatment can be embarked upon. I have never seen it done for seriously disturbed patients.

If all omens are favourable and a time has been agreed upon, the patient is sent to his parental home to assist with the preparation there, because "his hands must be in it."

All ceremonies take place during weekends. On the preceding Thursday, the healer who is to conduct the ceremony, members of his household, patients and trainees move to the patient's homestead and occupy a hut which has been set aside for their exclusive use. The first thing to be done is to prepare sorghum beer. Traditionally, it should be prepared from home-grown and home-grounded sorghum (but this is rarely the case these days) and the process should be started by a "daughter of the home," i.e., a blood relative, one who shares the ancestors of the patient. Strict supervision is exercised by the healer.

Here one encounters the first real and symbolic usage of nature. The sorghum is a product of nature, of Mother Earth. The process is one of fermentation and transformation from earth. In addition, the clan ancestors participate in the process through the hands and activity of a clan-linked woman. Apart from the fact that the brewing of beer is traditionally a female occupation, the female here seems to have a symbolic significance. The feminine element of the psyche, the soul, must be actively involved.

A canister of this beer is taken by the head of the household and left overnight in the cattle kraal in the area favoured by the ancestors–opposite the entrance gate. It seems to be both an offering and a message to the ancestors, inviting their participation. "Beer calls the ancestors."

After having been left overnight, it is collected early the next morning. It is claimed that cattle present in the kraal never upset the canister or drink the beer.

The acceptance of the invitation by clan ancestors is indicated by the white head of foam and the fact that some spilled over on the manure. The ancestors of the homestead and the beer, cattle, manure form links in a chain to which will be added the ancestors of the officiating healer. The foam and spillage is a sign to the healer to proceed. His ancestors and those of the family now "form a firm working relationship, assisting each other in the work for the patient."

That day is spent preparing for the rest of the ceremony. A large number of visitors can be expected and beer for their consumption must be prepared, using the beer from the previous day to start the process of fermentation. In addition, ordinary food must also be prepared. There is, however, no slaughter except for chickens.

The next day, Saturday, is the important one: it is the day on which the Ancestors of the River are to be consulted.

Everyone is awakened by the sound of drums in the darkness of the early morning hours. This creates a powerful effect; it involves one in the mystery of Africa. Before dawn, the emissaries who are to consult the River Ancestors are prepared. This group, the "river party," consists of two males and two females. Occasionally it can be a group of six or eight. A senior member of the healer's group is the leader, plus a trainee. The other two are relatives of the index person. In complete silence, their faces are covered with white clay; they dress in white, wear white beadwork and cover their heads with white cloth. This white attire serves as an indication of their identification with the Ancestors of the River, who are described as being white with long blond hair. The white paint on their faces serves as protection; for the Godhead, the numinous Ancestor of the River, may not be encountered unmasked and face to face. Thus attired, they walk in silence in single file, carrying their offerings to a pool in the river where the ancestors are to be consulted. At first light, they assemble at the river's edge and pour the offerings, one by one, into the water, intently watching what happens to each, and how those that can float move on the surface. These items are beer, white beads, tobacco, sorghum, seeds, pumpkin and calabash pips. A gripping atmosphere is created by the absorption and intensity of their concentration combined with the wild, natural surroundings, the sounds of early morning bird life and the rippling sound of the stream.

The reverence for, and communication with nature is unmistakable. Barriers between nature and human beings are broken down, and for a while, a unity is experienced which borders on the sacred. Time and space lose their boundaries and one shares in a ritual of immense antiquity. The spirits of nature have not only been consulted, but have been permitted to enter one's being and do their work there.

The party returns as it came, in an orderly single file

and in silence. At the homestead, in the space between the main hut and the cattle kraal, the arrival of the party is awaited by people who have also maintained a reverent silence. The silence is broken by the members of the river party giving the healer a detailed account of events at the river. The healer usually asks questions for more information or illumination of unclear or incomplete facts. When he is satisfied about the positive response of the ancestors and indications of their approval of the work and acceptance of the patient/trainee, he instructs his assistants to proceed. The index person's head is decorated with "white head beads" and his face is smeared with white clay. After the ancestors have first been served by pouring some on the ground, his new status and the success of the mission is sealed by everyone drinking neat brandy or beer.

The rest of the forenoon is spent in a festive atmosphere with much discussion of the events of the morning. The patient is now a member of the healer's group instead of spending his time with his relatives in their place.

During the afternoon, an intlombe is held, i.e. a vumisa (a divination session by a healer) is done to consult the ancestors about the future of the patient/trainee and his family of origin.

The second River Ceremony is called the fukamisa which means brooding, like a hen sitting on a clutch of eggs. There are significant differences between the two ceremonies.

In the fukamisa, the link with nature is even more clearly portrayed, and there are important symbolic features not present in the first. It seems to indicate a more integrated ego, and a psychic state which is receptive to increasing complexity of experiences and responsiveness to greater numinosity.

There is usually an interval of several months, even a year or more, between the two ceremonies. It appears that the experience of the first one must be fully integrated before the second can be embarked upon. Again, the timing for the ceremony depends primarily on the dream messages from the ancestors and the readiness of the family.

There is an important difference in the second ceremony, which is the isolation of the patient/trainee. At the first ceremony he sleeps with his relatives until after his acceptance, then he joins the healer's group to share their sleeping quarters. In this ceremony he is isolated in a hut for two nights and one day. He sees and talks with no one. He is fed on cold, salt-free gruel, which is passed through the door.

At dawn on the appointed day, the river party sets off as in the first ceremony. The initiant, however, is released from his hut, wrapped in a blanket which covers him completely, including his head and face. The healer gives him ubulawu (a herbal extract which calls the ancestors and opens one's mind to their messages) to drink to the extent that vomiting is induced. His body is also cleansed with a herbal extract. Thus mind and body are purified. By using his hands as a spoon, the healer then feeds him as though he were a newborn baby. The food consists of a thin porridge to which has been added a powder derived from the bark of a tree growing on the edge of the river, the dwelling place of the ancestors. All this is done in complete silence. On the return of the river party with a favourable report, his head is uncovered and the proceedings are as with the first ceremony.

With the second ceremony the individual is considered strong enough to withstand isolation and introversion, and to face the powers of the unconscious, the "wilderness within." The porridge with the powdered bark from the river tree is a symbolic incorporation of some aspects of the Ancestors of the River, i.e., archetypes from the collective unconscious. This presumably requires a degree of ego integration.

The period spent in isolation in the hut, brooding and facing emerging aspects of the psyche, is followed by a symbolic birth. He emerges like a newborn wrapped in a blanket, must be cleansed internally and externally, and fed like an infant. It is a lovely portrayal of a rebirth or birth of new awareness or new potential.

During the ceremonies, there is a constant combination of, or interaction between spirit and nature and the products of Mother Earth, and also between the ordinary human being and suprapersonal forces, thus creating a kind of cosmic relatedness. It is a process of transformation which arises from the unconscious through the activation of the archetypes and submission to their power by the human being.

The priest (in this case, the indigenous healer) invokes powers which are derived from the universe and "he commands these powers, because through arcane symbols he, in a certain respect, is invested with the sacred form of the gods."[2] The Xhosa healer can exercise this power for a variety of reasons. For the purpose of this article, only relevant ones will be mentioned.

The healer has profound respect for the powers inherent in nature and the universe, psychic elements as personified by the two kinds of ancestors and for human beings: "You will never become a healer unless you have learned the meaning of respect." His awareness of the importance of equilibrium, i.e., psychic equilibrium is the driving force behind the performance of rituals and ceremonies. The main aim of these ceremonies is to establish or maintain contact with the ancestors and to restore harmony where previously disharmony or even chaos has reigned.

The healer is constantly sensitive to meaningful manifestations of nature around him. For example, rain on a festive occasion indicates the goodwill of the ancestors; the call of a particular bird can be either a good or bad omen; the behaviour of wild or domestic animals also conveys messages. There is a constant interaction between nature, the outside world, and his own intra-psychic experiences.

The being of the healer is open to the power and activity of symbols. He does not understand these in the conscious Western way, but it is not necessary for a symbol to be verbally explained to be comprehended; it is often understood at a preconscious or even unconscious level by the people from whose culture it arose. The alien observer "must first crack the cultural code," to quote Victor Turner,[3] before he can draw conclusions about their meaningfulness.

The correlation of macrocosm-microcosm is not known to the people of Africa. According to Victor Turner, there is a widespread distribution of the theme, "that the human body is a microcosm of the universe."[4]

Finally, I would like to quote Paracelsus: "Everything was created in One, macrocosm and Man are one." Meier comments—"This was his basic conviction and it most probably accounts for his worldwide success as a man of medicine, for he always tried to bring about this macrocosm-microcosm harmony, loss of which, ac-

cording to him, accounted for his patients' sickness."
This accords with the Xhosa concept of health and the
good life.

As Jung says: "In his world spirit and matter (nature)
still interpenetrate each other and his gods still wander
through forest and fields."

NOTES

1. Heraclitus as quoted in *The Mysteries*, Joseph Campbell, ed.
Princeton: Princeton University Press, 1978, p.102.
2. C.A. Meier, this volume, p. 16.
3. Victor Turner, *Drums of Affliction*. London: Hutchinson
Library for Africa, 1981, p. 8.
4. Victor Turner, *The Forest of Symbols*. Ithaca: Cornell University
Press, 1981, p. 107.

Rix Weaver

7 *The Wilderness*

Oh wilderness have I not yet reached
your centre.   LAO TZU

Let us commence our wilderness walk in the rain forests
of far North Queensland, in forests alive with the freshness of lush green growth, the home of animal, bird
and insect of superb beauty. It was through this forest
that men of progress were putting a road which would
destroy the habitat of the creatures so dependent on it–
creatures that would soon become endangered species.

An analysand dreamed:

I am in a house, there is a knock or call at the door. I realise
I must go and speak with this person and sort out the rela-
tionship. I go around the house to another house, next door.
There is a group of people sitting at a table in the yard–two
men and two boys.

'I have come to see who's calling me to establish our rela-
tionship,' I said.

'She is over there on her own,' they said.

I go around a corner of the house and find a girl. We talk
for a while and I realise that there is an intimate closeness.
Then she leads me up a ladder which is leaning against a
high brick wall. At the top, I am terrified, feeling terribly

precarious. I cannot let go of the ladder. She walks along the wall in front of me and seems to drop down into the wall, where she has a secret cubby-house. She seems to be encouraging me to follow her.

'I can't do it, I seem to have a caliper on my leg and I feel precarious. Go and get help. I can't get down,' I shout.

She climbs past me. Help comes and I get down. I'm so glad to be on the ground again and I feel an immense sense of relief. Then she tells me about when the leg was crippled—as if it were hers—although I feel the story as if it were me.

'I was high in a tree in the tropical forests....I then began to actually experience the story taking place. I couldn't get down and they ran for a big piece of plant machinery to come and rescue me. As I saw it coming towards me, smashing through the forest, I realised that it was too massive to see me and would trample and squash everything. For a moment I was hanging by one leg, my crippled leg. I knew that if I stayed any longer the machine would gather me up with the vegetation and kill me—here there was a deep feeling of sorrow at the destruction of the forest. I saw the huge yellow machine ripping through the forest, accompanied by an enormous thrashing, writhing snake, as though the snake were part of the machine. Then I realised that I had to get out of the way, so I jumped from the tree to the forest floor and hurt my leg; but I did manage to get away from the machine's teeth.'

This is a dream of an analysand who lived for some time in a rain forest area that is now being destroyed. Physically, we, also, are trying to escape from the onrush of the great machine of progress that bears down on us; a machine of progress that not only destroys the wilderness with its ecological balance, but also whose soul is mirrored as the "concrete jungles" rise around us and the virgin and creative forests disappear. The outer world reflects man's soul, and if he has ignored Mother Nature, who is dependent on him for conservation, he has ignored himself. If he goes unthinkingly ahead with destruction, something destructive is happening to him. Man cannot tolerate too much interference with the psyche without becoming negative. Similarly, the forest gives up producing its magical world before the onrush of civilisation. Such is the mirroring of man, and the nature of which he is a part.

"Who is calling me to establish a relationship?" Is that not the question of today? To answer it, we have to realise the pain and agony of the primeval forest, to know it as our own.

Great stretches of wilderness lie on the southern land of Australia, from the tropical rainforests of the far North East to the wilderness of giant trees and luxuriant undergrowth of the South West corner. Dividing these lands is the living, surging wilderness of the desert. Man, who, unlike all other animals of the planet, carries the mystery of consciousness, has not known that "out there" is really "in here." He has not realised that the wilderness without and the wilderness within are one. What he has sought is progress, this man who has so brilliantly tamed the primeval forest to his needs. For such a long time, dark-skinned people lived in the forest, taking its fruits, its animals, and the fish of its rivers as their food. They paused to plant back yams and they preserved the young.

The balance of nature was real. From within, from the heart's sure knowledge, they were informed. Call it *participation mystique*, call it instinct–it is all that. Call it, if you will, nearness to the original intentionality of the creative dawn.

Today roads sear those forests, changing the lifestyle of bird, insect and animal; many are killed as mines yield up their treasures from an age-old land. The orchid that flowers beneath the ground and whose delicate petals lift a mound of earth above, is the forebearer of the wide variety of brilliantly coloured ground orchids that flourish in the West state. This orchid, blooming unseen, is the link with the ages: it is the archetypal reminder of a One continuum, unchanged, that includes all multiple expressions in itself, the possibilities for everything that has emerged. Scientifically, we would point to mutations. But even the most highly developed gradually make way for progress though they may be as forgotten as the soul of man. They are treasured by those who realise that to neglect them is to neglect the soul, for humankind alone can change the world at which it looks.

Rich with possibility and creativity, both outer and inner wilderness respond equally to the face man turns to them. We feel we have come a long way from our remote so-called beginnings; yet the ever challenging wilderness of unknown reality has moved away from us. "We must move forward," we say, grasping riches from a planet yielding us diamonds and gold, uranium and oil.

I am going to take you again from the remote southern corner of Australia where the damp cold rain forest flourishes, across to the wilderness of the northeast tip where the tropical rainforest, in its lavish beauty, supports a great variety of animal, bird and insect life. Between these two forests is a desert that is also a wilderness. It is a desert of the sort crossed by ancients bringing their messages to mankind–messages emerging from the inner wilderness, the rich virgin world of the soul.

I am reminded here of Moses' forty-year journey in the wilderness. This journey, one could say, was the physical unfolding of the imagery of the promised land. Moses made an enormous journey: everything was pointing to a different style of life. To arrive at it, it was necessary to journey through the wilderness. Our lifestyle, in comparison, is a paradise. We have the promised land which was imagined by them. Through that inner image, Moses performed the miracle of the parting of the waters. The soul, whose wilderness is within, supports outer reality; it creates the image.

As Moses and his followers found order and intentionality within, they worked through the outer desert. There were no signposts in the outer wilderness except for the stars, the sun and moon. Nor are there signposts in an inner world. Yet within is a psychic wilderness containing everything that can be known, including the inspirations and ideas that can serve as signpost and guide.

The tropical forest has its problems. Streams rush down mountains and over rocks, waterholes abound beneath a canopy of trees which are draped with twine upon twine of creepers, and are hung with orchids and ferns that provide homes for nesting birds. Will the brilliant birds still fly and sing when the road goes through?

How can birds nest when their familiar regions are destroyed? In that tropical area, I have seen the white cockatoo come every night at the same time to the same tree and leave at the same time each morning. For generations these birds have known no other home. There are thousands more like them—creatures and insects upon whom the forest, the wilderness, depends, as they depend upon it. The mighty ash of cooler forests depends, for example, on the mound-making of the lyre-bird. All are One in the Creator's plan, in the ecological balance which man has so much failed to recognise.

Let me repeat: "out there" is the mirror of "in here" and the reciprocal roles of soul and matter, psyche and soma become unbalanced at our expense. The wilderness is Mother Nature, who has placed her abundance at our disposal as custodians of the earth. The "wilderness" mirrors man's attitude toward his soul.

Is this planet falling before the axe and the soul of man? Is a barren world becoming lost to the real meaning of creation? The message of the shrinking wilderness is clear; the lesson of its complete balance, its economy and ecology is a Bible without words. It is the face of the Creator and a call to mankind who carries the possibility of really seeing what this world and man himself are about. Only when the creative potential of the inner wilderness is realised will the global wilderness be allowed to flourish and the earth allowed to breathe. Can we not learn to balance the needs of man with the needs of the planet that supports him?

Jane Hollister Wheelwright

8   *The Ranch Papers*

After my father's death in 1961, the family spent six and a half years liquidating 38,000 acres of land and other holdings belonging to the Hollister Family for generations. During these years I was driven to try to understand what had been going on for more than a hundred years of family ownership. Because there were no precedent-forming guidelines for such an inquiry, or at least none to my knowledge, it was necessary to follow a certain spontaneity that consisted mostly of thoughts bubbling up by themselves. Whenever I was in contact with the properties this spontaneity was deepened by memories which stubbornly insinuated themselves and gave the properties a certain validity.

The special, spiritually meaningful (and often destructive) impact of the place was obvious. I proved it by my behavior, as did others in the family. The only certainty during that difficult period was my vague conviction that without a recognized context one's life has no meaning. Without some understanding of the land that raised me, I knew I would be a kind of nobody–

someone lacking in purpose. To grasp the extent of impact, both good and bad, was not therefore merely an exercise in speculation. It became more and more a necessity as the prospect of liquidation of the land loomed.

The fantastic beauty, the ruggedness, the physical uniqueness and the cruelty of the ranch lands certainly meant something. We were touched more deeply than we ever suspected by a land that was not always a loving, embracing earth-mother kind of place. We knew that beautiful place could also have harbored fear, or feelings of revenge or hatred.

Tied in with my sense of place were disorganized, subjective, but potent reactions asking to be recorded. It was as though someone, undoubtedly my psychological self, was telling me that the more they were honored, unruly as they were, the more these reactions might reveal their secrets. This was not easy because they came into my head forcibly, like bombardments. Confused and groping and nearly always embarrassingly sentimental, they continued driving me to jot them down in the small frayed notebook that soon became my constant companion. In no time, it was clear that the messages came only when my wilderness context and I were alone together. Then life and meaning joined, giving off a vibrancy that I had not known before.

I wondered about the power of the ranches over us— an early and wholly unconscious imprinting on each member of our family inevitably had its effect—but there was no one to talk to about it. Certainly no one was concerned in the same way as I was.

As I roamed the privacy of hills and mesas and canyons in a kind of farewell to my wilderness home, I slowly arrived at the most important conclusion of all, namely, that I must go my own way. To go my own way, however, meant interpreting the lands in understandable, communicable, and assimilable terms. That would have to be my tortuous way to independence. I would have to evolve by sustaining the impact of the lands in order to be free of them. But how, specifically? In poetry, paint, words? That was the biggest question. Because of my compulsion to take notes, the medium would have to be language. To find the telling words I had to proceed blindly. I would have to bear with the chaos and the undifferentiated jumble of feelings turned loose by the threatening prospect of losing our lands. I would have to believe there were ordering forces in the offing that would help.

With this in mind I began to write The Ranch Papers, one chapter of which I would like to present in the following pages in honor of C.A.Meier.

The Ranch Papers: Chapter xii

A deluge during the night made planning for the day useless. Two inches of rain had fallen as the forecast had predicted–imagine a two-inch sheet of water laid out on 38,000 acres! Over leisurely cups of coffee I thought of my good luck in escaping back to the ranch in midafternoon despite the prevailing dark and forbidding mood. I also relished envisioning the scene encountered on the way, especially the Mexican cattle gathered on the mesas in all their odd shapes and colors–many more than in the early morning. Some of them were milling in bunches on the road in continuous restless movement. Others seemed even more vigorous than in the morning: now grabbing at food on the trot; rudely pulling grass up by the roots and quickly, neatly, nibbling yellow mustard flowers. They were demonstrating what had happened to the yellow effect on the range that year. Individual animals taking their stand on the road held their own against me, making butting gestures at the car.

The last of the cattle out of the high back country overlooking the home canyon poured down the precipitous fronting hills, hightailing it through the heavy sage, kicking, jumping, sliding. Like the others in the early morning they were wildly, dangerously playful. They were also moving to the mesas where the great blue herons had gone the day before in anticipation of rain. These birds were our only truly reliable weather forecasters.

In the night, rain and wind slapped against the board and batten of the superintendent's little house. The eucalyptus over our heads whirled round in violent, erratic, mad dances. Distant breakers and still more distant thunder added to the confusion. Rain, wind and breakers combined their fury in a roaring turmoil throughout the night. There was some comfort in this pandemonium, for without a doubt it insured a good year of plenty for man, beasts and plants.

Listening to the storm I had time to reminisce about our seacoast. I thought of the breakers, whatever their intensity, as indicators of how things are along that coast. They are also conveyors of messages from distant lands which take up the pressures from foreign storms thousands of miles away and expend them against our cliffs. The ocean sets limits to all the surrounding elements with its own voice. So alive, it is like a faithful companion, a protection in the night. The moon too, had been reflected in the wide tidal swings that were occurring.

That night of violence was only a variation on the

theme—the ocean's other side. It comforted me in my snug hideout, promoting my sleep.

The rain finally ceased by daybreak. But the minus tide would not turn from its extra high until late morning, so there was no use venturing out. The superintendent advised against a ride inland because the horse could never make it on the soaked trails. Reluctant to offer advice, he said in a near whisper, "Let the ground settle itself down a bit before riding to the beach." The ground had a life of its own! A familiar note—animism perhaps—but it seemed more like the natural feeling of a man whose intimacy was with the place.

Later in the day, I found out what he meant. The ground, oozing, swollen and shifting in the saturating water, was treacherously undermined. My roan slipped and slid, his four feet going in four directions at times. It was strange to see a horse so helpless. The old feelings of *terra firma*, the solid reliability taken for granted, all that one associates with the ground under foot, were no more. There were no little islands of safety. That was my first conscious encounter with hostile land. It reminded me of the bottomless bogs and quicksand experience long ago in small estuaries formed by our larger creeks. I looked back with more awareness to the day our Indian pony sank to her belly, my brother and I hauling on the reins, forcing her to fight her way out. We were too young to fully grasp the horror of that predicament.

I could not remember ever having experienced a quarter of a mile like this—and it was all because I had wanted a safe ride on the beach. The earth clung in masses to my shoes, sticking in heavy lumps of adobe we called "gumbo mud." I nearly gave up.

The ocean was not much more inviting. It churned

and swirled and reared. Muddy run-off had turned it to a light dull brown. Mud still flowed from every stream, out of every culvert and indentation in the land. It streamed out of scalloped crests topping the banks as hundreds of tiny streams seeping down their fronts.

A continuous, broad band of yellow foam formed as breakers and swells piled up. There was not a square inch of quiet water anywhere. The tide had turned only because the tide book said it would. There was a telltale thin strip of raised sand, no longer reached by the waves. Storm pressures were still driving up the water.

In all this turmoil, the small snipe were running with deliberate movements along the contours of the waves as they ebbed, each time catching whatever was left exposed. Calculatingly they ran just out of reach of the incoming waves. A natural law was in control. They were tiny bits of order within the unruly, law-breaking atmosphere everywhere.

To the west the sky was a heavy gray with ominous black masses of clouds which lay directly in the line of our progress. A cold and wettish wind came from that quarter like a thrust. Was a second storm brewing? Better not think about it! Besides, there was the blue sky to the South and East which promoted wishful thinking for one bent on a long ride.

White cotton clouds still hovered over the range, but they were rolled back on themselves by the wind. Down the coast, eastward and as far as the rounded green hills of the Alegria Canyon, the background was gray and almost blotted out. The perfect, almost semi-circular hill-tops which always so pleased the senses now stood out sharply green against the gray.

Earlier storms had completely denuded the beach at the

headlands. There was nothing but rock underfoot and the deluge of the night before had once more scraped them clean. The exposed rock ledge which ran from the high yellow earth banks to the wild water where it sank out of sight, had a curious man-made, chipped look, as though leveled off by short chisel strokes. Centuries of wave action had done that.

My roan preferred the ledge to the sand dune into which he tended to sink. He sniffed suspiciously at the smaller deposits in the rock. With frank disapproval he cleared them in wide, unexpected lunges. He spooked at the tiny earth slides from above and shied at every insignificant pebble rolling down the bank. He had a special distaste for the minute cave-ins on the small sandy banks of streams traversing the beach. His jumping and snorting finally got to me, infecting me with uneasy feelings and foreboding. The horse seemed particularly focused on something in the high, saturated cliffs. He continually pulled away from them. Land slides? Strangely he did not fuss at all at the piles of debris and mounds of kelp on the shining, slippery rock under foot, nor did he mind the splashing waves.

The roan never stopped trying to get out of the situation and double back for home. He had more sense than I. I had to exert all possible pressure to keep him moving forward. On hindsight, I am sure he was disturbed by the black horizon that should have disturbed me.

Around the next headland, and past more rock ledges, we edged along a narrow pass against the bank where the waves were still smashing at the bits of white sand that were left there. Underfoot it was soft but not impassable; the roan snorted louder than ever.

Suddenly, the cold wind in our faces doubled in force,

and with no warning clouds blacked out the sun and everything around us! Single fat raindrops fell in the bitter stinging cold; and then came the downpour. My mackintosh, which was made for fishing, not riding, only came to my knees. The horse slowed to a standstill in spite of my forcing. We endured for some minutes–then somehow the rain was no longer wet. It had turned into large hailstones that bounced off both of us.

Pandemonium hit the breakers. The streams of water flowing out of banks swelled to twice what they had been, and new ones were breaking out everywhere from places never before associated with water. Breakers darkened into deep brown with the mud. The earth, rocks, water and mud broke loose as though there were no moorings left. Over it all were the wild cries of shore birds. The drenching continued, intermittently relieved by hail. My shoes filled with water and my jeans were soaked from the knees down. The horse dripped water, his ears drooped dejectedly.

There was one alternative to our predicament; turn back and try to reach home. But I was not in my right mind: this was perhaps my last chance to face squarely into a storm–to indulge in what few civilized people ever have the opportunity to experience any more. It was also perhaps a recognition and a farewell to the elements all in one. Besides, why shouldn't we rise above it and sit it out as wild animals have to do?

I knew that horses in pasture back their rumps into a storm when it drives too hard, it is warmer that way. It was, and the roan calmed down a little. We hugged the bank to escape the whipping wind, in spite of the eerie sense that something high up should not be trusted. The roan's suspicious behavior had undermined me or possibly my own sensitivity was sharpening. Without the slightest warning a torrent broke out at our feet. Old Roan recoiled and so did I. A solid flow of yellow rushed by. A long, wide, solid streak sped across the clean gray sand into the yellow ocean foam. It did not belong there.

Contamination of the ocean and beach by mud cuts across one's lifetime's sense of difference between sand and earth, in spite of their common origin.

We would have done better on the sheltered side of the next headland. Where we stood was too much in line with the gale, but to move at all was arduous. The horse seemed to agree with me; it was better to stay put, in spite of the beating.

The wait gave me time to register a mixture of feelings. There was first the foolish feeling for not having noted the black warnings in the West, but over and above that was the exhilaration that came from bearing out the crisis to its end. It felt good not to be defeated–so far. The sense of achievement in so wild a situation made me part of nature, part of all life. It was a chance to look out at Nature from inside her. The wetness was reassuring too, proving once more that soaking bitter cold does not harm you. I was able to forget for awhile the endless man-made devices in one's daily city life that are designed to keep you not fully alive. Overall was the need to experience the violence of the wild once more, perhaps for the last time, and, if possible, take a little of it with me, to make it a permanent, knowing part of my whole.

The drenching may have lasted half an hour, and was followed, again with no warning, by a blazing hot, glaring sun. The shore birds, particularly the killdeer and the willets, which had yelled throughout the squall, were suddenly silenced. A solitary blue heron still faced the direction of the storm, but this time his neck pulled in. Snipe flew low over the foam, bent on some purpose. Many tiny beach flies stung me. The impact of their minute, solid bodies had the force of hailstones. They swarmed out of nowhere to be in the hot sun which played upon the warm steaming banks.

Several times black clouds gathered threateningly in the west, announced each time by bird cries. Now that the storm had subsided, I could look around, and the wetting no longer mattered because of the heat.

Redwinged blackbirds were already dotting the sand. They were out of place, like the vultures I had seen on the beach at La Paz. Their conspicuous markings and shrub-loving characteristics did not fit that setting. They were like people flocking to the beach on an unexpectedly sunny day in winter. The glistening green-black birds, with their startling red wing spots edged in yellow, sang ineffectually and incongruously against the breakers. Their songs were an odd contrast to the killdeer alarms, which are thin and shrill but synchronized, punctuating the drama. Gulls were in formation, flying low over my head in a slow white relaxed orderly way, enjoying the hot sun and the sudden quiet.

It was already past noon. In the East, great white clouds billowed in force. One dark rain cloud, apparently in the process of releasing some of its load, loomed up again in the West, this time like a gigantic hand. The thick wrist rose on the horizon and the fingers reached into the clear blue sky. It touched an eerie cord deep down in me—ominous, but somehow with meaning. We were directly in its path yet still in the hot sun. The atmosphere was clear, the visibility nearly perfect. The clarity of the air drew close the objects around us like a magnet. Visibility also heralds a storm; yet what about the thorough scrubbing we had just had?

Beyond the San Augustine Cove, the headland had melted into a confusion of yellow earth–into shifts and slides loosened by the saturating water. One mass that had slipped was still leaning on the cliff face. Caves, cracks and holes opened high up in the precarious jumble. Piles of earth were strewn over the sand. Old bench marks from ancient ocean levels on the cliff still barely showed. Much of the coast line had been chewed off and washed out to sea. All in all, as on land, it gave a sense of impermanence and insecurity.

Old familiar sand dunes normally piled high against banks and cliffs were gone, leaving only small sand deposits here and there in crevices and corners out of reach of the onslaught of waves. The cement flume for the pipes laid out to sea for oil and gas was exposed, forming a barrier across the beach. Two days before you could not find it.

Flocks of godwits, their light brown color warmed in the sun against the white and gray of the many other species, were concentrated on the beach. The warm color tucked under their brown wings blazed into red when they flew. Cousins of the curlew, they stalked around like miniature storks with their necks pulled in.

We continued up the beach in the direction of Punta Concepción nearly as far as the Little Cojo Cove. Large rocks stuck out of the sand and shallow water in a strange wild row. Old Roan once more sniffed and snorted and tried to turn back. His fear got to me. The minus tide which by now had receded to its low, seemed to be fulfilling some dark planned purpose in exposing what lay beneath. Black shapes strangely reminiscent of the eerie menhirs of Britanny jutted from the flattened breakers. Ocean water churned white at their bases. The largest rock of all, a boulder, was set apart from the series. It barely surfaced, its bald top glistening. To this the roan said "No," and he circled around it warily, snorting loudly. He would not be forced. For such a stable, sensible horse, his fear and distrust of the rock surprised me. But I was sympathetic—it was indeed the head of a submerged monster.

Looking for giant limpets, I dismounted and examined another rock in the shallow water. I had to reach the rock in the infrequent intervals between the biggest waves. Climbing up, holding the reins with my free hand, I caught several limpets before they clamped down with their forty pound thrust. The knapsack for the shells somehow had to be kept from falling into the water. It was a balancing stunt on the slippery surface, made more so by thousands of tiny jets of water from sea anemones. There was always the danger of being washed off. The suspicious roan thought I was crazy. His complaints were continuous. Each breaking wave sent him swinging round and round the rock. The deep water splashed over most of the rock and welled up to his cinch band. He could have reared, falling back on his reins, and broken free, leaving me to walk the seven miles home.

By then, we both had had enough. As we set out for home, relief showed in every movement of my horse. His ears pricked forward and a spring in his gait described his optimism. His anticipation of home promised a long, peaceful journey for me. My only concern was the threat from the black cloud looming in the distance and moving towards us. The visibility also increased suddenly. Out at sea, a freighter's bow and stern were visible. Its middle section appeared as though it were below the water, meaning the ship was beyond the horizon.

The rain cloud to the West came unceremoniously toward us, but, by some undeserved luck it came only as far as the breaker line at our feet and then veered quickly back out to sea. It came and went a second and a third time. Its abortive charges gave me, finally, some feeling of immunity.

The willets refused to fly away unless we came right up to them. They seemed only mildly afraid of us. In flight they revealed striking black and white markings. Broad black velvet was laid on to a background of white. The few times they left the sand they flew in long sweeps over the breakers and came to land not far in front of us. They always kept to the same flight pattern. Finally, at the end of the cove, they doubled back and settled in peace behind us.

At three, and right on time, I heard the familiar gig-gedy-jog of the orange colored train "The Daylight," as it slipped over the rail joints. When it came into sight, it was as if it had been caught in its own private life without the usual fanfare and fuss. Its engine sounded a very long dragged out "O" at each crossing. It came along effort-lessly and rather slowly; it seemed to belong, and did not jar the feeling of the coast in the slightest. The rhythmic noises of the train recalled my childhood, when we had no other way of telling time, and the sound of one in the distance meant we were hopelessly late for our lunch.

Puffy mounds of pure white foam, left by the outgoing tide, skidded slightly on the wet sand as we approached the home canyon. But behind us, as a constant companion, was the great black hand full of rain, looming ominously against the surrounding sky of clear, bright blue, its wrist still resting on the western horizon. The long, dark fingers of the hand now stretched directly overhead, angling across and far down the coast in the high wind. Out at sea, rain fell at intervals from the dark, thick, slanting streaks of the cloud's fingers.

The eerie, meaningful feelings I had had earlier later resolved themselves into the memory of a Biblical passage which had to do with Elijah's confrontation with the pagan prophets of Baal, who challenged him to prove his god by ending the drought. Later, when I looked it up, I found Elijah prayed to God, while at the same time commanding his servant to look for signs. After the seventh try the servant said: "Behold, there ariseth a little cloud out of the sea like a man's hand . . . the heaven was black with clouds and wind, and there was a great rain."

The afternoon sun was low in the West, lighting up the mist that rose from row upon row of churning breakers, like rows of charging herds of phantom horses, their manes flowing in the wind. The mist had refracted the light in a way that intensified and magnified everything. The softening effect of the mist enhanced the brilliant green of the long, thin fringe of grass topping the cliffs and banks.

To the East, there were a few low-lying black and troubled clouds. The hand never left us. Overhead its fingers continued to stretch and veer outwards to the sea. Far out to sea, a few clouds, lit by the sun, piled up like miniature castles and towers. The shapes were delicate whirlwinds that pirouetted; otherwise the sky was cloudless.

Dark green seaweed showed in the minus tide, and streamers of green brightened the brown kelp. Foam sparkled and popped on the sand as the sun lowered almost to the sea's horizon. In it were yellow, pink and green lights that shone like diamonds. The foam scudded a bit in the slight wind; some of it went out on the tide.

By five o'clock it was quiet enough to hear the small birds in the brush on the low banks. Only the breakers stirred. All else was serene in the long shadows. The horizontal evening light brought out the white of the churning water, making it glow in the mist that was blown out to sea from the turmoil.

Big shore birds were very much in evidence. Walking as though performing a stately dance, they moved their necks exaggeratedly like East Indian dancers–back and forth, not side to side. Among them were round-bodied, black turnstones. They were black and white with long black vests. The little snipe, shining white and no longer nondescript as they had been in the stormy over-cast, were busy with their supper.

Creeks tumbled out of the very large culverts under the track's right-of-way. By then I was walking to get the stiffness out of my bones, so I had to remount the roan each time we came to a stream in order to cross. My saddle was weighed down with a sack of abalones and my knapsack had to be treated gently, because it was full of frail shells. With my stiffness, mounting became a chore. After the first sprightly move towards home, the roan resumed his jumping each time a pebble rolled down the cliff. He snorted at the few tiny mudballs and cave-ins made by the streams rushing across the sand to meet the incoming tide. At each crossing he lowered his muzzle, sniffed at the water, groaned and sighed miserably.

But, as yet, no complaints about the ocean! Apparently he was not going to forgive me for the morning's huddle against the cliff.

One last look to the West in the path of the setting sun revealed miles of churning breakers, their mist and foam lifted high. It was a lovely vista, tender and luminous, extending to infinity.

The broad band of moving white water along the breaker line curved gracefully with the curve of the coast. It extended all the way to the sun, which now rested on the water. Breakers beyond breakers were topped, softened and lighted in an unbelievable unreality, blending the broad scene.

It was a magical landscape, a grand subject for a painting or a poem, if it was not overdone. Such an interpretation might be the means to hold onto its import, but for me, the wild beauty was not communicable. It would have to be held in memory and perhaps it was all the richer for that.

We were ushered around the last headland by the few remaining rays of the sun not yet lost to the sea's depths. They were exactly at the point of being cut off by the horizon, but in the last moment they lit the small, smooth pebbles scattered over the wet sand, making each one a tiny lantern in the black. The shore was carpeted with softly glowing lights, like those of fireflies.

It was dark on land when we climbed up at the home canyon. The big clouds behind the Bulito sentinel hills were a curious smoking color. They were massed and softened at first sight, and rounded. In no time, they took on something of the seashells below them, more salmon than pink.

It was hard to let go of the sight in order to open the

stiff gate at the tracks, but I had to hurry because black night was about to descend. Twilight is very brief at this latitude.

A last look at the sea was barely possible but essential. The familiar abalone colors had surfaced and the sea had calmed. It was as though it was ready at last to be put to bed by night.

The drama that was there that day was something to talk about yet, paradoxically, there was a stronger need to be silent. It was too personal a matter to discuss, and the others sensed this when I reached the house. The superintendent merely said, "We thought about you during the cloudburst." No questions were asked. They somehow knew the experience on the beach was part of a personal farewell to the land of my beginning.

Laurens van der Post

9   *Appointment with a Rhinoceros*

*Wind and the spirit, earth and being, rain and
doing, lightning and the awareness imperative,
thunder and the word, seed and sower, all are one:
and it is necessary only for man to ask for the seed
of his being to be chosen and for the sower within
to sow it through the deed and act of himself, and
the harvest for all will be golden and great.*

THE SEED AND THE SOWER

I met C.G. Jung and C.A. Meier and their immediate
world when I was still technically and mentally a soldier
in uniform. My own war had lasted almost continuously
for ten years because, on my release from three and a
half years in a Japanese prison, I went straight back to
active service, and for many urgent personal and public
reasons that are not relevant here, I was compelled to go
through another kind of war caused by the proliferating
forces of nationalism in revolt against imperial masters
in Southeast Asia and particularly Indonesia. My war
service had been so long that I had more than a year's
leave when at last I returned to Britain. On the long,
roundabout way of my return to Britain, I had an experience of the natural world of my native continent of Africa
that was to influence my postwar life profoundly. I shall
deal with this experience in its proper place at some
length, but it is necessary to emphasise here at the beginning that, although its impact and consequences were
most immediate and revelatory, the meaning of the
experience itself, and its objective implications for us

all, would not have orchestrated in the manner it did if it had not been for this experience of the immediate world of Jung and the meeting and long friendship with C.A. Meier which followed.

I had gone to Zürich to join my wife Ingaret Giffard, who was studying at the Jung Institute in Zürich of which Dr. Meier was the Director. Along with Toni Wolff and Jung, he was her principal guide and mentor. I was naturally drawn into this remarkable student world focused on the Institute. And, to the extent that I could do so while continuing my own writing, I attended many of the public lectures. For the first time in my life, I read the work of Jung and his circle and realised how much I had missed by not doing so many, many years before. I also got to know Jung and spent many hours alone with him, finding in the beginning that we were talking almost as much about Africa as his work in psychology. I remember, indeed, many exchanges of experiences and ideas about Africa, in which Jung frequently referred to it as "God's own country" and "the last continent with a soul of its own." I discovered with delight that, of all his many journey's in search of objective evidence for his far-reaching hypothesis of the collective unconscious, his African journey and his stay among the Elgonyi not only provided conclusive testimony, but gave him the greatest joy. I remember him writing to me once to thank me for a book I had sent him, because it "brought back those already remote memories of thirty years ago ever so vividly: unforgettable colours, sounds, perfumes of days and nights in the bush." It concluded: "I am grateful to the particular genius–*vultu mutabilis, albus a et ater*–that took it upon itself to weave the pattern of my fate, that it included the experience of Africa and its glory." His insight into what

I had come to think of for many years as "my" Africa was so profound and acute, that at times, I felt almost angry that he should understand it even better than I did, and would tease him to the effect that he was not really Swiss at all, but an honorary African. This invariably made him laugh in that elemental way of his, which compelled me to add: "You see! You even laugh like a Bushman," and he would laugh all the more.

I soon began to realise that in the Africa he and I recognised there was a special relevance for the world of analytical psychology. I remember one long discussion with C. A. Meier about this natural relationship that seemed to exist between the great interior of Africa, which was my home, and this vast objective "within" of the soul and its universal dreams in which Meier was guide and tutor at the Institute. In fact, the relationship was so obvious to him that he and Jung persuaded me to give some public talks about Africa at the Institute. I remember that the first talk was almost entirely about the animals of Africa, and I was struck at the manner in which the whole natural world, which in a sense I had taken for granted, instantly took on a deeper meaning for my audience than it had for me. As a result, I discovered an inner necessity to explore this world for myself and in my last week in Zürich I tried to formulate some preliminary testimony, drawn from my own experience, of how the interior of my part of Africa, which I had seen so vividly and lovingly from without, when seen from within was singularly continuous and at one with this world with which analytical psychology was concerned in so revolutionary a way.

Although it is many years since I gave that talk, its essence has been so much a part of my postwar evolution, and has contributed so much to the atmosphere of my long friendship with C.A.Meier, that my memory of it is, I believe, as accurate as it is well-nigh total. Obedient to an old Zulu maxim that the longest way around is often the shortest way there, and inspired by the look of encouragement from C.G. Jung, who sat with his wife Emma directly in front of me, I began my talk somewhat to this effect: "Dr. Meier, Ladies and Gentlemen, whenever we look at the history of man, particularly the history of Western man, and, more particularly, the history of Christian man, we see man in search of a self: the kind of self that is not obsessed with the external world, but a self that honours both an external world and an internal one. This self is aware not only of the past and present, but also has a sense of direction. It attaches the utmost importance to the process of becoming something more than it happens to be at any given moment in time. And it is this element, in the midst of being, of becoming a more fully aware expression of all the life that has ever been and bringing something new into the light of our time, that gives, or should give, man his dynamic and his greatest value."

In the beginning, this self was sought in groups and in great collectivities, but it is as if it gradually dawned upon man that the self cannot really be found in groups. In fact, groups and numbers can be a peril to this kind of self that man is seeking. What he is really looking for is a kind of self that will be a specific expression, a specific call or vocation, and that will be in a sense the carrying on of a personal mission. It is a personal story in life that must be specifically realised. The truth and the meaning that we find in seeking such a self must stand intact, no matter what the collective and individual pressures against

them. This seems to me a singularly Western kind of
concept, which has been present from the Greeks onward. The creation of an individual of integrity who
will resist all the negations of a collective value in the
interests of the community itself–the community for
the moment being ranged against it–is to me one of the
most precious values of our heritage. Indeed, we have
seen throughout our history that this has been our quest,
expressed legally from the time of the Magna Carta
onward in our concept of the rule of law, Habeas Corpus,
and our concept of an individual conscience. Our history
makes unique and profound sense only when seen as a
search to create a specific man, a man who, in his life,
as Christ did in His, makes some great universal and
cosmic value specific in his own nature and stands fast
on its behalf regardless of the pressures he may face.
Without such a seeking, life has no meaning. Hence
Hegel could say, before Christ there were only peoples,
and after Christ, for the first time, there were persons.

Yet strange as it may seem, the very first people
already had an instinctive sense for this sort of meaning
to life. If I had to say, therefore, what I think is the
greatest difference between this moment in which we
stand and the time of space and mind of the descendants
of the first people of the world–the bushmen who still
live in the natural surroundings of the desert–it would be
the following: the man in the desert who is nearest to
man in the beginning, as I know him, feels that wherever
he goes, he is known; wherever he goes, he belongs.
We feel that we *know*, but how much do we still feel that
we are known? How much do we feel that we belong?
The answer, sadly, is that there is a kind of desperate
loneliness creeping into the heart of modern man, because

he no longer seeks the answers of life with the totality
of his being, in both dimensions of world without and
world within. He is going back to a collective concept
and surrendering this precious gift, this ancient opportunity of being an individual who is specific for the sake
of the whole, an individual who believes that a union of
diversity, a union of individuals who are different and
specific, is truly strength. A grey, abstract, impersonal
organisation of a materialistic civilisation is pressing in
on us and eliminating these life-giving individual differences and enrichments in us. Everywhere we are increasingly being governed according to purely materialistic principles: principles which are interested in us
only insofar as we have uses.

This is by the day more true, even in the Africa of
which I wish to speak, the Africa which fathered Sir
Thomas Browne's profound observation on Renaissance
Man: "We carry with us the wonders we seek without us:
there is all Africa and her prodigies in us."[1] I was speaking many years ago to an old Zulu prophet who, when
I asked him about their First Spirit, 'm-kulunkulu, said
to me: "But why are you interested in 'm-kulunkulu?
People no longer talk about him. His praise names are
forgotten. They only talk about things that are useful
to them." This is our plight today as well. Reverence
has been lost for this individual whose self is greater than
the individual who serves something inside himself that
is a microcosm of the great wheeling universe. This
individual, who, by being himself, is in a state of partnership with an overwhelming act of creation and is
thereby adding something to life that was not there before. This has been taken away from us, and we no longer
feel that sense of belonging to life. In the depths of

ourselves we tend to feel abandoned and alone. This is part of the sickness of our time.

Human beings can endure anything except a state of meaninglessness, and it seems that a great tide of meaninglessness is creeping down upon us, and that nothing but conformity will do. Take, for instance, a concept about which we hear so much: the statistical concept of the average man. When you come to think about it, there is no such thing as an average man. The average man is like the average rainfall. It is the one rainfall that never falls! Because numbers have replaced unique and human considerations in the faceless abstractions of our time, we feel lost in the world. Nobody cares anymore for what we are within ourselves, but only for our functions and usefulness to them and their societies. We cease to care in return.

One of the most awful consequences is that, as we lose touch with the natural man within, which demands a unique self of us, we lose respect for him. And as the natural man within loses honour, so too does nature without. We no longer feel reverence for nature, and end by exploiting it.

There is a story about this individual quest which the Stone Age people in the desert tell and it is, in some way, a natural parable to me. It is the story of the young man and the lion. They say there was a great young hunter, perhaps the greatest they had ever known. Now the hunter is an interesting figure, because he carries a symbolic charge. He is not only the hunter in the world without, who seeks food for the body; he also represents in the human imagination that aspect of man seeking new meaning in the jungle of his time. One day when this hunter was on his way to the water, a lion, which was also on its way to the water, attacked him. This happened because for a moment he had ceased to be fully aware. It is interesting that this is the fatal sin, that fate always acts through our lack of awareness. It is also interesting that both were on their way to water, because waters in the desert are places of magic; they are places where the desert is transformed and new life grows. Here, as in the Bible and most myths and legends, water carries an image of new being, of new life. It is as if the story is saying: Both the lion and the man are in search of a new form of life.

The lion seizes the young man, but, being very thirsty, it says, "Well, I won't eat him at once." The young man knows that his only hope is to pretend he is dead. So the lion carries him off to a thorn tree and pushes him into the fork of the tree. The thorns stick deep into the skin of this young man, but he knows that he must not show his pain. Nonetheless, the pain is so severe that through his closed eyelids tears start to run down his cheeks.

Then an extraordinary thing happens: The lion starts to lick the tears of the young man, and instantly the situation changes. It is a marvelous moment of revelation, right at the beginning in the mind of the first man, of the role of tenderness, of gentleness and of compassion in life. The lion feels changed and says, "This young man whose tears I've licked is my man forever." And the lion goes slowly over the hill to the water, deep in thought.

The moment the lion is gone, the young man jumps up and runs back to his community. The community, because they are very fond of him, jump up in alarm and ask, "What has happened?"

He tells them the story and they say, "Well, don't worry. We'll defend you against the lion."

But he replies, "You won't be able to defend me against the lion, because it has licked my tears and will insist on coming for me."

Nevertheless, they wrap him in all the hides and skins they can find, and prepare for battle. The hide and skins are, of course, symbols. They put him back into a collective attitude, a collective state of mind.

I would like to emphasise at this point the importance of the lion. The lion, not only in the imagination of first man, but even in our day, is not the king of beasts for nothing. It is so chosen because, of all forms of animal life, it is the most many-sided, the most highly differentiated. It is powerful. It is swift. It is strong. It can see as well by night as by day. Its senses of smell and hearing are very good. It is very intelligent, and it doesn't abuse this formidable combination of powers. It has a sense of proportion, and does not kill except for food. (This latter is a well-known fact in countries where lions have not deteriorated as a result of being hunted and tormented continually by tourists.) Above all, the lion is fundamentally the cat that walks alone. In other words, the lion is the individual; it is the symbol of the instinctive and royal individual self.

In the story, looking for a man to eat is a way of acquiring new being, because primitive man believed that whatever you ate, you became. So it is in certain symbolism of today. In taking communion, for instance, in taking the bread and wine, one partakes of Christ's flesh and blood in order to become like Christ. Similarly, at another level, the lion, by eating a man, seeks to become man, to be also human. This is what the story is saying to us. The greatest, the most formidable combination of instincts in the command of life demands an individual man, demands also to be lived individually.

But the young man runs away from this fate. It is too much for him, and the community agrees with him. They try to protect him. In a minute, however, the lion appears. They do everything they can to kill it, but they fail. The lion simply lets it be known, "I've come for him whose tears I've licked and I shall not go away until I've got him."

At last, the young man says, "Look, it's no good. The lion will kill all of you." He makes them take the skins off him—he undoes the collective attitude to the problem—and he falls in front of the lion. The lion then falls upon him, and the story tells us that both in that moment die.

The fate of lion and man would seem to indicate that, although primitive man feels that the attainment of the self must come about, although this is what life is for, it is not fully possible as yet. It is still to be achieved sometime in the future. Nonetheless, it is something for which we must earnestly begin to strive. Never before has it been so important to rediscover this natural pattern in ourselves, to withdraw from the collective values, or lack of values, of our time, and to find ourselves in our unique, historical, specific and individual way.

I was just emerging from a time when I, too, had lost contact with my own natural self. I had had more than nine years of war behind me and only recently had been summoned to report to the War Office in London for an urgent consultation, because a crisis had arisen in a part of Southeast Asia, where I was representing the British Government. I got as far as Cairo, where my plane was refueling, and as I walked about to stretch my legs at the airport, I spotted a South African military airplane. Suddenly I found myself feeling terribly lonely. I thought, "I've not seen anybody from that part of the world for nearly ten years. I'll just go and see who's in the plane."

By some extraordinary twist of fate, the person in charge was somebody who had been in school with me. So I said to him, "Brandt, you wouldn't give me a lift south, would you?" And he said, "Come on; jump in."

In a sort of daze, not knowing what I was doing, I found myself going to the control tower and sending a telegram to the War Cabinet. Although I was what is technically known as a senior officer, I wasn't so senior as to be doing this to the British War Cabinet! I sent a telegram nevertheless, saying that I couldn't come to London immediately because an emergency had arisen, and that I would explain later. I didn't then know precisely what emergency and I didn't know how I was going to explain. Indeed, I thought I would probably be court-martialed on my return.

In any event, I got into the plane, and some days later landed in Johannesburg, South Africa. I went to a hotel my family had always used where I knew the proprietor. He nearly fainted because when he had last read of me in the newspapers some years before, I had been reported, "Missing, believed killed," and as far as he was concerned, the news had never been corrected. However, when he had recovered, I swore him to silence, again purely instinctively, because I really had no clear idea as to what I was doing and what I would do next. Indeed, I was rather like a sleep-walker. But in the night something must have happened to me, because early the next morning I woke up and knew what it was I wanted, or rather, had to do.

I went out and hired a truck, got some guns, ammunition, and food supplies and two Africans to help me, and before the great city was awake, I was on my way north to one of my favourite parts of the African bush, wedged between Kipling's "great greasy Limpopo" and a magical river called the Pafuri. By this time, I was exhausted and bewildered, but I have never forgotten the moment of my arrival, precisely at a place sanctified by associations of many years. Here I intended to camp, between the dense riverine bush and a long belt of fever trees. So long had been my separation from this world, and so improbable was it that the journey behind me would ever have allowed me to see it again safely, that I had a feeling as if I were recovering and rediscovering in a nightmare of sleep a blessed release into something I thought lost forever. In the long, level light of a winter evening in the Tropic of Capricorn, the fever trees had gone all green and gold, and the bush all along its black outline against one of Africa's mythological sunsets was loud with the song of birds making music out of their homecoming. And in between the bush and the tall fever trees, colonnaded and arched like pillars in a cathedral, the long, tassled grass did a deep obeisance to the evening air. Not far away I heard a leopard starting on its prowl and a bush buck, the bravest of the brave, answering it with a defiant bark.

As I stepped away from the camp and the fire which my African companions had lit, and walked slowly down towards the river through a scene that glowed more like some ancient illuminated manuscript than a rough African camping site, a movement ahead stopped me. Out of the bush, on a footpath leading to the river, stepped an enormous kudu bull with horns so tall and wide and heavy that only pride enabled him to keep his head in the air. As I saw him, he saw me, and he stopped without any trace of alarm; over the spangled grass we stared at each other. He was outlined against the sun. I could not have wished to see him posed more clearly or beautifully, but I was blurred against the dark of the bush behind and he was forced to throw back his head and to sniff the evening air between us. He did this long and unbelievingly, and in a manner which almost, in a state of heightened perception, seemed to suggest that he had known me but never expected to see me again, and could not believe his senses. But suddenly, it was as if he knew, and his spiral horn was lifted suddenly with a heroic sweep; he became manly and erect again as he slowly and unperturbedly resumed his journey, passing within a few yards of me without a trace of alarm or condescension, but in a matter-of-fact way that was implicit with kinship.

And then, it was as if all the chains of a kind of slavery dropped from me with such a rush that they tinkled and rattled in my imagination. Suddenly I had finished with the war, and a great rush of emotion swept over me that was impossible to describe except that all its urges and manifestations met in a wordless cry, "I have come home!"

As a result, I stayed in the bush for three weeks, and lived there with my two African companions and only the animals around us. Day by day, I seemed to become more human again. During all those years when I had been able to view nature in the jungles where I had fought, even though my eyes were telling me how beautiful it all was, no corresponding emotion was being transmitted to my heart. Now this detachment was all abolished and a new order seemed to be introduced into my being so that everything I saw was once more felt keenly and vividly. Indeed, just then, all was felt with such an agony of reality that it was almost as if I was seeing nature and life for the first time. It was as if all else between me and this privileged progression of a new order of harmony had been the hallucination and delusion of a fever—a terminal sickness of soul and meaning of the world that had produced the war.

By the end of the three weeks, I felt I had begun to become an individual self again, so reestablished contact with a lost and natural man in my soul, that I was strong enough to face the world and people again. I thought of Swift's remarkable parable of the Kingdom of the Horses and his description of Gulliver's return at the end to his own beloved home and family, and how at first Gulliver could not endure the sight or smell of men or even of his wife and children. He had to bed down and stay with the horses in the stables and ration himself to tiny little outings and brief spells with his family. Gradually, he became used to their smell and their reality again and finally one day he was able to return to the world of what we so mistakenly call "ordinary men."

I remembered also how the old Zulus, who were a military nation, always had a rule that when any of their armies returned from war, the men were not allowed back into the community until they had gone through a ritual of purification. This ritual of purification, which was very intense, was designed to take away the spirits of death and killing that they brought with them from war. Only when they had been purified were they allowed back into their communities.

It was as if the bush and the animals and nature had done precisely the same for me. At the end of three weeks,

I felt as if I, too, had been purified of the war. I had ceased to be a number and had become a more or less human, individual person again. Only then was I free to go home and greet my mother, whom I had not seen for eleven years. I could not have done it before; if it had not been for the bush and the animals, I could not have done it at all. Paradoxically, we may take this story as a form of proof that it was perhaps the right thing for me to do, that it was the right way of doing my duty: for not only was I not court-martialed, but I was offered promotion instead!

What I have just described is an illustration of one of the many paths we can travel in order to rediscover this lost self. Somehow we must recover reverence for nature. This materialistic, industrialised life of ours has taken this reverence away from us. We must stop using and exploiting nature and go back instead to the man who lives in partnership with nature. This does not mean that such a man is blind or unaware. It simply means that he does not use nature for any slanted or trivial purpose.

Those people who wish to preserve what is left of the natural world should go into the bush or some other wilderness area as I did. When one walks into such country and sees creation as it was in the beginning – untouched, unspoiled by the hand of man – it is as if one were walking into a great temple or cathedral. It is extraordinary how the capacity for religious experience comes back to one there. Unless we recover this capacity for immediate religious experience, we will be unable to find this self of which I am speaking. Fewer and fewer of us can find it in churches, in the organised religions of our time, hard as we try, and much as we admire the churches for what they do. Many of us would have to say that while we find admirable examples there, we do not find the direct, living experience of religion. But when you get into the bush, or into any stretch of unspoiled nature, you will find animals that still glisten and are as vivid as if they had just come from the hands of whoever created this mysterious universe of ours. They are acolytes and priests, as it were, of the first temple of life. As one walks with them there, one feels a nearness with the Creator and the first pattern of creation, which restores and renews one.

In this regard, I have a deep feeling that in the beginning, we were much nearer to the animals than we are now. A state of communion existed between us, a kind of correspondence that we have lost, but can nonetheless regain. This was demonstrated to me once while I was making a film in the interior of Africa. As always in the bush, I had observed a rule of silence as if it were one of the most sacred commandments of the bush itself. A commandment that ensures silence is not broken except when compelled by some necessity of life and being of nature. When we ourselves had to speak, we learned to do so almost in whispers because there is no sound that carries further or grates so much on the nerves of the bush as the human voice. As a result, we became so intimate and at one with nature that we filmed lions without telescopic lenses. There was one conclusive moment in fact, when I was able to walk, unarmed, to within a few yards of one of the most dangerous animals in Africa, the rhinoceros. He had made several dummy charges at me on other occasions, but on this early morning, when we had both barely come out of our sleep and the grass and the leaves were all pearl and silver with a heavy dew, I came upon him sunning himself in a little clearing which might have been tapestry for some legendary lady of the unicorn.

It was one of those rare timeless moments charged with a meaning uniquely its own; and it added to the light of the sun and a glow as of gold made mist that was not of the there and then. An extraordinary feeling of harmony and of belonging was implicit and magnetic within it, and the rhinoceros was at the centre of it. I felt a foolhardy desire, as it seemed to my conscious self, to do something to express a strange inrush of gratitude for that privileged scene by going nearer the rhinoceros and somehow to make it clear that human beings were not just guns and violence, that somehow we too needed that sense of belonging which emanated from him and the bush. I whispered to my companions to stay where they were, stopped and told them what I intended to do. They tried hard to dissuade me. The armed ranger who officialdom had insisted was necessary for our protection on this particular occasion, was especially urgent and implored me not to go forward. I did not realise at that moment that he himself, some years before, had been tossed by a rhinoceros and spent nine months in hospital before he was fully recovered. Nor could I foresee that afterwards he would be physically sick, because in what followed, I was between him and the rhinoceros and he would not have been able to shoot had he charged me. Still, however, I had this feeling that some sort of recognition and significance of the meaning of the moment was necessary, so I walked slowly and evenly towards the rhinoceros. He turned slowly about to face me squarely, lowered his massive head so that his wide chin practically touched the ground and his scimitar horn was pointed straight at me. He was, as the meaning of the moment that is synchronicity demanded, not a black, but a white rhinoceros.

I went steadily towards him until I was a mere three yards away. Then it was as if a signal passed from him to me that I had gone near enough and now had to observe what there was of distance left between the two of us; distance from there on was a matter of identity and dignity. I stood still and looked as steadily at him as he looked at me. He belonged, of course, to one of the oldest forms of mammal life. His species goes back to the age of the dinosaur and pterodactyl, and many hunters regard him as one of the most dangerous animals, one of the ugliest and most removed from any vestiges of animal reason. Yet, as I stood and looked at him there, I thought I saw through all that was considered inelegant and ugly in his appearance. I saw a strange first essay on the part of creation in the pattern of animal beauty, and the impact of this breakthrough in prehistoric aesthetics was so overwhelming that it was as if I had never encountered anything more dazzling on earth. With it all came, as a bird on the wing, the realisation that the hand and fingers which had modeled him so magnetic and at the same time so solid and enduring and strong in paradoxical marble, were the same hands that had modeled us. Suddenly it was as if not only the gap of what we call time between him and me had been closed, but that a powerful feeling of emancipation was illuminating my war-darkened and industrialised senses.

I thought of an apocryphal gospel which had not long been discovered. It is one of the oldest gospels to which we have access in its original form. In it, the disciples had asked Christ the question asked also in the New Testament: "How shall we know the way to the Kingdom of Heaven?" Most of us know how Christ answers it in the New Testament, but in this apocryphal gospel he answers it differently. He commands them: "Follow the birds, the beasts and the fishes and they will lead you in."

I had no doubt then that by opening our imagination to the beauty and diversity of life and proportion of all the kinds of things that surrounded me in nature in Africa, nature would unlock a way towards a form of wholeness which we are compelled to find within ourselves if we are not to perish. It is a wholeness that surpasses and transcends all the paradoxical, contradictory and apparently conflicting necessities of life: a self wherein we see as in a mirror a bright reflection of the author of creation within and without.

So that morning and through the days that followed, the rhinoceros walked at the head of a long procession of animals that by the day seemed more and more to me pilgrims on an evolutionary journey of time that is a measure of the abiding and as yet unfinished business of creation.

It was after some such fashion that I would finish my first attempt in public to appraise this mysterious interdependence of world within and world without. In private, however, and above all, in the silence of night when alone with myself, it was not the end of the matter, because all that the rhinoceros represented was not static, but alive and dynamic and increasingly evocative, less instinctive perhaps and more conscious in its questioning. And this is not surprising. As already implied in all that has been written before, it is as if a kind of cosmic symbolism is made manifest in the world of nature, and night and day seeks to inform our spirit of new possibilities of being and meaning. Not only is it symbolism infinitely diversified and rich in form and colour, but it is almost as if it were

the act and deed of the symbol itself. It is so designed, perhaps, not only to increase our awareness of ourselves and
the universe, but also to enlarge and heighten consciousness of creation itself. Once the symbol has conveyed all
that it encloses of hidden and unrealised meaning—as the
seed within the earth, its grass and flowers—it is transfig-
ured into living life and form, and all that gave it a butter-
fly beauty within ourselves and our imaginations falls
away to make place for another urgent symbol charged
with a meaning that is still to be discovered and lived. It
was natural, therefore, that once I had an instinctive
inkling of the symbolic significance of this procession of
animals, I should ask myself, also consciously: "But
why the rhinoceros? Why did he and his twin, the unicorn, play so great a role in the transformation of myth
and legend into human behaviour and living quest? And
why, if an animal with horns were necessary, had it to be
just one and not two chosen from amongst the resplendent
and elegant antelopes of the bush and savannahs of my
native country, of which there were some one hundred
and forty different kinds spread between the Cape and
Cairo?" The clue to some sort of an answer came to me
from something Adolf Portmann once told me. It was to
the effect that, of all our senses, the sense of smell is perhaps by far the oldest. And the sense of smell, I had
already come to suspect, in all the roles allotted to it in
the animals of the stories of Africa, represented intuition.
It was a capacity built into all forms of life to make them
be aware of invisible aspects of reality that the keen-
est sight and the most acute form of animal hearing
could not divine. It was a sense that saw, as it were, not
only round the corners of time but also through the
opaque past behind us, and made the natural walls and

limitations of the apprehensions of flesh and blood trans-
lucent with light beyond. It was the faculty in St. Paul
which made him define faith as the evidence of things
not yet seen. It was the preliminary awareness of the "not
yet" and "the now." It was the golden thread which
linked the first act of creation not only with the present
but also with the last. The word is feeble as such words
are when used to denote a movement of spirit that is without beginning or end. But this whole process of evocation
started with a wondering about the imagery of the rhinoceros in the darkness and silence of an Africa where one
could hear the stars—and a dreaming self, convinced that
intuition was at the beginning as it would be at the end;
that indeed, it was elemental in that leap without looking
out of the darkness of chaos and old night into the light of
day which we call creation. It followed as the day the night
for me, therefore, that without it, creation would have
had no sense of direction. It is at the very least the great
cosmic gateway, if not the high road itself. So the rhinoceros at the head of my private and personal parade of life
made profound symbolic logic. It is an animal whose eye-
sight is poor; his hearing is better and even extraordinarily acute, but his superior, supreme sense is that of smell.
In the realm of symbolism, therefore, he is as profoundly
a realisation of intuition made flesh and blood as there is
to be found on animal earth. And from there, my imagination in time seemed to discover the reason for the choice
of a single horn among all other forms of horn and antler.
Those lovely spirals of horn, for instance, that graced
the head of the kudu which had greeted me on my return
to the bush, on grounds of strength and sheer beauty
might have been a more desirable candidate for a symbolic
role to an imagination obsessed merely with externals.

On consideration, however, those horns were connected to the head of the animal, which housed not only the brain, but a complex of senses such as seeing and hearing which are focused on the demonstrable and the rational. They appear to have come later and, suggesting a more advanced state of consciousness, were set above, perhaps dangerously high above, this first living instrument of smell that was intuition. Only the rhinoceros and its kind possessed, in addition to their expertise in smell, a formidable horn which grew naturally on the nose and so was, in a sense, a fortified sense of intuition made manifest.

I know many stories of animals with a capacity for seeing in the dark and finding their way by smell, who play heroic roles in the drama of the everlasting conflict in which intuition is embroiled, in order to make another leap forward in life and awareness. They invariably represent the more tender, delicate, caring, trusting and loving ways of advancing the cause of intuition, because in the natural stories of Africa, the role of intuition is by infallible instinct the most diversified and honoured of all.

Indeed, some of its most heroic protagonists are among the smallest and most vulnerable forms of natural life. In the stories of the first people of Africa, for instance, this role is made Homeric in the smallest of mice and exalted in the porcupine. It is made immortal in the image of a little bird, which is ultimately destroyed by man over and over again because it will not let the conscience of creation in man sleep, but is constantly resurrected to make its admonitory voice heard in the depths of the bush, darkening the narrow winding footpath of consciousness which brings man out of the dark forest and vast plains behind him into this enigmatic and endangered present. But in the rhinoceros alone is the intuition armed and made strong enough to do battle against its enemies, whose physical brutalities are hurled against intuitive realisation in the here and now.

The horn indeed is to intuition and the animal who embodies it, what Excalibur, the great sword, was in the Arthurian legend. The sword is not only a weapon in the physical world but it is also an image of discriminating awareness hurled into the battle for wholeness which the search for the Holy Grail represents. The rhinoceros is a pre-historic image of the Parsifal, his horn, the dedicated sword, to the animals on this evolutionary pilgrimage.

This, finally, is the image of animal pilgrims I brought back with me from the bush. It is a visual exhortation to the human spirit of how intuition, too, needs to be armed with far greater awareness than we, with our slanted and lofty forms of consciousness, are prepared to give it. It is a testimony of promise also of the singleness of the resolution of the opposites, which other forms of horn in the animal world proclaim: the abiding promise which makes the spirit steadfast in pursuit of the loftiest aspirations constantly pressed onto it in unending abundance by the master intuition that is part of the act and deed of all creation.

There is much more that I could say, but I hope that this is enough to explain at this particular moment why the rhinoceros continues to walk with that incredible easy and resilient step at the head of my own private and personal procession of animals, reaffirming the pattern of metamorphosis and transfiguration in all living and natural things, and evoking the same transcendent sense of direction which his mythological brother, the unicorn, evoked in both the Western and far Oriental spirit.

NOTES

1. Sir Thomas Browne, *The Urn Burial*, Frank L. Huntley, ed. Illinois: Harlan Davidson, 1966.

Sam Francis   (*with an excerpt from* Goethe)

10   *Nature Aphoristic*

Nature! We are encircled and enclasped by her—powerless
to depart from her, and powerless to find our way more
deeply into her being. Without invitation and without
warning she involves us in the orbit of her dance, and
drives us onward until we are exhausted and fall from
her arm.

Eternally she creates new forms. What now is, never
was in time past; what has been, cometh not again—all is
new, and yet always it is the old.

We live in the midst of her, and yet to her we are alien.
She parleys incessantly with us, and to us she does not
disclose her secret. We influence her perpetually, and yet
we have no power over her.

It is as if she founded all things upon individuality, and
she recks nothing of individuals. She builds forever, and
destroys forever, and her atelier is inaccessible.

She lives in her children alone, and the mother, where
is she?—She is the sole artist; from the simplest material
she passes to the extremest diversity; with no hint of
strain she arrives at the fullest consummation—at the ex-

actest precision, always veiled in a certain obscurity.
Each thing she makes has its own being, each of her manifestations is an isolated idea, and yet they all are one.

She is Whole. To herself she metes out reward and
punishment, delight and torment. She is austere and tender; charming and horrible; impotent and omnipotent.
All things are evermore in her. Past and future are nought
to her. The present is her eternity. Gracious is she. I laud
her with all her works. She is wisdom and tranquility.
No answer to life's riddle can be wrested from her, no gift
can be extorted from her which she does not offer of her
own free will. She is full of finesse, but her goal is good,
and it is best to avert the mind from her craft.
    She is perfectly whole, and yet always incomplete.
Thus, as she now works, she can work forever.
    To each man she appears as befits him alone. She cloaks
herself under a thousand names and terms, and is always
the same.
    She has brought me hither, and will also lead me hence.
I yield myself to her in trust. She may do with me as she
pleases. She will feel no hatred towards her work. It is
not I myself who have spoken concerning her. No–it is
she who has said everything, both what is true and what
is false. She is guilty of All, and hers is the honour of
the Whole.

–*Goethe*

Translated by Agnes Arbor,
Chronica Botanica, 1946.

O Nature! O Wilderness!
I have picked the shoot
I have killed its glory.
When I was young
I planned nothing
I did nothing
I thought nothing
But I saw His Beauty in Nature.
This Beauty is more fleeting
than the waters and more
lasting than the great
magnet of space.
We see it in the
laws of Nature.

We see Nature as unpremeditated and that is its link to
art. Unpremeditated art must be part of Nature itself.
Every detail of daily life is a perpetual blessing. Artists
work to show this to everyone. It is an unremembered
act of kindness and love to do this.

Contact with wilderness means to me a new beginning,
a new understanding of what *the beginning* means. It also
means unleashed energy available here and now. And so
it means connection to the creation of the cosmos. Without this relationship there would be no continuation of
the creation of the cosmos for us, for we are engaged
willy nilly in the cosmic creation as it continually unfolds.

The Wilderness gives me access to power, in the psyche,
in the trees, in the stones, in the stars. It is a field of
power. We are recharged in the magnetic field of the
wilderness. I find the will to be wild, the will to be

original in myself. We are here to marry the wilderness
to culture. Water and wine are so mingled, so wedded,
as soul and spirit; a point of light that speaks to me.

Nature is the blood of the universe
streaming in the firmament,
not one drop to be lost.

In the wilderness God lies on a leaf in the form of a babe.
And yet he's on a leaf in the form of a glowworm, whose
tiny light fills the cosmos. From this we can see how to
fulfill great Nature's plan. We kill Nature in our misery
and with each killing misery comes again into the world.
No matter how minute the killing, killing means love
wasted; wasting is the misery of our world. It means
killing the spirit, it means wounding the already wounded
great soul. It comes from not paying attention to the
Wilderness within. When we are in touch with the
wilderness each act is an oh so common miracle. The real
comes as a *miracle*.

Colors are stellar messengers.
Dawn converts us to love
in its pink flush.
A capacity to imagine is passion,
emotion, and image united.
Both being and image
are forever unbreakable.
Imaging then means facing that which descends
from within.
Gold and silver are malleable
together under the pounding of the stars.
They must approach each other

from within to unite.
Man and woman must do the same
for a union to occur, otherwise
it is merely a glazing over that occurs.
The angel brings images of the psyche
back from the farthest reaches
of the Wilderness within.
So united that we are always
filled and overflowing with this
densest water and volatile wine.
If the spirit overflows us, we race.
As a child I raced with the spirit
and was her companion. I learned to be
a servant of power. Wilderness,
all yearning comes from that darkness.

The Ohlone Costanoan Indians lived where I was born,
near San Francisco. They are coastal Indians and honored
the redwood trees and the owls as sacred beings.
Dreaming was a vital determinant in their lives. They
made ceremonies and danced on the brink of the world.
They were radiant people and lived in the sea of spirit as
the fish lives in the sea, enhanced, made alive by
the waters.

The first dream of God is the wilderness which he spreads
at our feet. Please let us tread lightly. Nature defines
imagination. As William Blake said, what can be
imagined is true. Images are immortal in imagination.
The earth is still there dreaming in that blueness. The
earth is still there dreaming in the forest and the prairie.
To consciously live in chaos is to live within perfection.
Perfection means the most possible relationships (an

infinity of relationships) made all at once without regard
to order. Order is always invisible. The myths are ablaze
in the night skies again. The myths come again and again,
as they have always done, in the darkness. They will
come again and again whether we survive as a race, or
not. They will come again even if we are freed from time.
The wilderness is my beacon. Angels are a forgotten part
of Nature and are messengers of the one imagination
carrying visions, terrors, sorrows all in the form of images.
Space and time are relative to matter, not to imagination.
Time is the mercy of infinity. Imagination is not subject
to the laws of time and space, but to the laws of the psyche,
laws of which we have only an inkling. Creation of the
wilderness was an act of mercy–if it can be thought of
as an act.

Questions to Nature:
Who is there?
Where did I get this gold
band on my mind?
What is the matrix of the mind?
What lies there, his bones like teeth?
How did the flower find
just this eye socket to blossom?
Who is he that takes the
bit of heaven in his teeth?
Who smiles in the dark
this golden laugh?
What has the fangs
of order in the dark?
What is your answer
of answers to the question
of questions?

Why not bend your knee?
Rejoice in the freedom of that law.

My heart associates these images with wilderness:
Circumference within–center without.
Walking hand in hand with Basho
through the bush.
The eye of the Eagle
is darker and much deeper
than the sound of the bleating
lamb.

The call of the loon
ricochets off a tiny pebble
I hold.
The loon's call is contrapuntal
to the singing of the wolves
floating over that hill.
I will know the coming of spring
by the sound of my own voice.
I am a small little stone
that disappears into the
universe of stones.
I am steering by the torch
of chaos and doubt.
I must set my knowledge
in my not understanding.
I found that matter followed
Nature in perfect obedience.
I found force is docile to wisdom
which makes eternal circles.
If properly taken science confirms
the dazzling conception that

the universe is in perfect obedience
to the laws of Nature.
The laws of Nature regulate all
rising, falling, spreading, moving,
winging, loving, blossoming, dying,
living, and are arranged
in Beauty. So science is the
study of Beauty.
Science could be a symbolic
mirror for supernatural truths.
Nothing is lost,
nothing is created.
Our work is a sacred activity
instructed by Beauty itself.
Beauty is a raging sea of fire
out of which the frail blossom
falls.
The order of the world is the
beauty of the world and is
invisible.
Beauty bites at my heart.
I am living with my bones,
they are still red.
This is Radiance.

CONTRIBUTORS

DR M. VERA BÜHRMANN, M.D. *Gansbaai, Republic of South Africa.*
Psychiatrist, transcultural researcher, and psychotherapist at the
Child and Family Psychiatry Unit of the Red Cross Hospital in
Capetown.

DR JOSEPH HENDERSON, M.D. *San Francisco, USA.*
Lecturer Emeritus of Neuropsychiatry at Stanford University,
Jungian analyst, lecturer, and author.

DR MOKUSEN MIYUKI, PH.D. *Los Angeles, USA.*
Professor in the Department of Religious Studies at California State
University at Northridge, Jungian analyst, and Taoist scholar.

DR C.A. MEIER, M.D. *Zürich, Switzerland.*
Professor Emeritus of Psychology at the Swiss Federal Institute
of Technology in Zürich, Jungian analyst, lecturer and writer.

DR IAN PLAYER, D.M.S. *Howick, Republic of South Africa.*
Founder of the Wilderness Leadership Organisation at Howick,
initiator of the World Wilderness Congresses.

COL SIR LAURENS VAN DER POST *London, England.*
Author, explorer, soldier, conservationist and filmmaker.

RIX WEAVER *Applecross, Australia.*
Jungian analyst, lecturer, and author.

JANE HOLLISTER WHEELWRIGHT *San Francisco, USA.*
Jungian analyst, lecturer and author.

SAM FRANCIS *Santa Monica, USA.*
Artist, filmmaker, founder and publisher of The Lapis Press in
Santa Monica and San Francisco.

DR ROBERT HINSHAW PH.D. *Zürich, Switzerland.*
Psychotherapist, editor and publisher of Daimon Press in Zürich.